EARLY PRAISE FOR *REACHING FOR SUNRISE: A WIDOW'S MEMOIR*

"How does love survive in the face of unspeakable tragedy? Lokita's immersion into the teachings of Tantra at least gave her some tools to traverse a landscape that nobody ever wants to have to pass through. How does love survive? One courageous step at a time evidently. Lokita needed to share her story with the world, and we all need to hear it. Remarkable."

— Will Johnson,
Author of *The Posture of Meditation*,
Breathing Through the Whole Body,
and *Rumi's Four Essential Practices*

"This book is the gripping saga of a woman's immense courage in the face of death - her own and the murder of her husband, both at the same time. She shows us, through her improbable resurrection that we can, against all odds, gamble for life, and life responds with moments of grace that are nothing short of miracles. A truly engrossing, riveting, and inspiring read."

— Margot Anand,
Author of *The Art of EveryDay Ecstasy*

"Lokita Carter underwent an unimaginable heartbreak during a time of hardship in her life; a series of gut-wrenching events that upended her world and sense of self. She tells the tale of surviving grief and pain with the same grace, love, and strength it took her to come out the other side. Her story is one of resilience—a how-to for not just withstanding the worst but emerging from the flames of hell with the ability to still hold love in your heart."

— Vivian Ho, Journalist,
Author of *Those Who Wander: America's Lost Street Kids*

"An utterly engaging personal account of making peace with extraordinary tragedy."

— Holly Rawson, LPC
and Brian Ahern, LCSW

"In *Reaching for Sunrise*, Lokita shares her personal journey with unwavering candor and authenticity. Through her story of loss, grief, and resilience, Lokita has deeply touched my heart; her memoir is a testament to the strength of the human spirit and the possibility of finding hope even in the face of great tragedy. An inspiration to read and behold."

— Martin Adams,
Author of *Land: A New Paradigm for a Thriving World*

"There are not many life stories that touch the heart as profoundly as this one."

— Dr C.J. Ladwig,
Ophthalmologist

Reaching for Sunrise
A Widow's Memoir

LOKITA CARTER

Reaching for Sunrise
A Widow's Memoir

Behind the High-Profile Murder
of Steve Carter

LOKITA CARTER

© 2024 by Lokita Carter

Author Photography © 2023 by Joachim Gern | Berlin | www.joachimgern.de
Photo of Author with her Dog © 2023 by Stephan Schaefer | Costa Rica | www.shepart.photo

All rights reserved.

No part of this book may be reproduced, stored in a retrieval system, stored in a database, and/or published in any form or by any means, electronic, mechanical, photocopying, recording or otherwise, without the prior written permission of the copyright owner.

To maintain anonymity, the author has taken the liberty of changing names and identifying characteristics of some individuals and places mentioned herein.

Excerpt from *Those Who Wander: America's Lost Street Kids* by Vivian Ho is used with the author's permission.

Design & Publishing Assistance by The Happy Self-Publisher | wwwhappyselfpublisher.com
Development/Brand Consulting by Logan Rose | www.loganrose.co

ISBN 978-0-9755511-6-5 Hardcover
ISBN 978-0-9755511-7-2 Paperback
ISBN 978-0-9755511-8-9 E-Book
ISBN 978-0-9755511-9-6 Audiobook

BREAKING NEWS

"The search is on for a killer in Marin County who gunned down 67-year-old Steven Carter on a popular hiking trail. Carter was out walking his dog when he was shot multiple times. Our ABC news reporter is live in Fairfax, California, with the details…."

By the time Steve's murder hit the national news networks, I was already devastated— beyond devastated—I was almost destroyed. At 3:30 on the morning of October 6th, 2015, four solemn-faced police officers sat me down in the dining room and one said, "Mrs. Carter, we have some unfortunate news." Nothing could have prepared me for what was coming next.

"The body of Steve Carter was found about 100 feet down beyond the entrance to the trail…"

"Your husband was found shot dead on Gunshot Fire Road in Fairfax. Your dog was also shot, but she is expected to recover," the police told me.

"Sadly, the victim was actually still holding on to the leash of his brown Doberman Pinscher, who had also been shot…"

It could have been anyone walking their dog that late afternoon—that's what made Steve's murder a national sensation. It could have been you, me, or the guy next door. It was purely random that it happened to be my husband.

"Sheriff officials say the victim's car is missing and probably stolen…"

"Let's kill the old man," they said, nodding to each other, and didn't even give him time to say, "Hey, you want my car? Here, take the keys!"

"Steve Carter was a prominent Tantra Yoga instructor. He and his wife founded the Ecstatic Living Institute in Lake County. A motive for Carter's murder is unknown…."

They shot him. They killed a wonderful man, the love of my life, and took him away from me when I needed his love and support the most. I was suffering from a rare and aggressive form of breast cancer and undergoing intensive chemotherapy. By chance, he had been picked out to die, and the odds were three-to-one that breast cancer would kill me, and I would follow him to the grave.

"Police are searching for two men and a woman who they say are persons of interest in the fatal shooting…"

From that moment on, it would take immense courage to choose to live because everything I knew about my life had been stripped away. My friends urged me to go on, but for what?

TABLE OF CONTENTS

Introduction xi
CHAPTER 1: Fresh Beginnings 1
CHAPTER 2: The Lovers Meet 9
CHAPTER 3: A World of Our Own. 17
CHAPTER 4: A Suspicious Spot. 33
CHAPTER 5: Accepting the Unacceptable 47
CHAPTER 6: Three Total Strangers 69
CHAPTER 7: Into the Fire 83
CHAPTER 8: A Time of Reckoning 97
CHAPTER 9: Facing the Accused. 115
CHAPTER 10: I Am Not My Breast 131
CHAPTER 11: Treatment & Testimony. 141
CHAPTER 12: The Great Escape 155
CHAPTER 13: Memorial & Meltdown 171
CHAPTER 14: Costa Rica Bound. 183
CHAPTER 15: The Final Court Scene 197
CHAPTER 16: Happy Endings 211

Epilogue 223
Acknowledgments. 229
About the Author 233
Stay In Touch 235

INTRODUCTION

My story, which you are about to read, is dramatic. It's about a woman who was living her dream, creating a beautiful life for herself, only to watch it fall apart as she contracted life-threatening cancer and tragically lost her husband to a violent act of murder while undergoing cancer treatment.

But this is also your story because during our lives, we all experience the same dynamics of creation and dissolution. We try to build the best lives we can for ourselves, only to watch them crumble and disappear sooner or later.

Life is constantly slipping through our fingers, changing as it does so. Nothing stays the same for long. All our attachments, which seem solid and permanent when we make them, are destined to be torn from our grip.

But there is light, even though loss is often accompanied by dark moments of grief and despair. In this book, I will show you how it is possible to be happy, feel fulfilled, embrace life, and experience joy even when challenged by the most terrible events.

Life is not against us. It may seem like that when we lose those we love or have to say goodbye to the lifestyle we created, but the opportunity to love life, love each other, and love ourselves remains fresh and undiluted.

This is the story of my journey. Let it inspire your journey, too.

Lokita Carter

CHAPTER 1

FRESH BEGINNINGS

It started innocently enough. A friend sent me a video, thinking I might be interested. *Interested*? As soon as I pressed the play button, I was hooked.

In a warm pool of softly lit blue water, a man held a woman gently in his arms. He slowly and gracefully danced her through a series of movements, stretching her out, sweeping her around, curling her into a fetal position, even taking her under the water for a few moments of total submersion.

The woman was relaxed, surrendering herself to the flowing movements. She wore a nose clip that allowed the practitioner to take her head beneath the water's surface. The dance of her body seemed effortless and enchanting.

As I watched, the excitement in my body told me that I also wanted this experience. The combination of sensuality and surrender gave me goosebumps. It reminded me of those special moments during lovemaking when two beings move deeply and harmoniously together, and sex suddenly becomes sacred.

I wanted to find out more about this water dance. Searching the internet, I discovered "Watsu," which I gathered was a form of shiatsu massage in warm water, similar to the video I had been watching. Soon, I came across a book by Harold Dull, the inventor of Watsu, and phoned his headquarters in California to order it.

I liked the photos and eagerly devoured the text. In this particular form of bodywork, the practitioner floats you in her arms, then moves and stretches your body while at the same time working with shiatsu and acupressure points. The warm water—heated to body temperature—provides a reassuring fluid medium reminiscent of being in the womb, offering a sensual, weightless, and utterly relaxing experience.

I promised myself to experience Watsu as soon as possible and already sensed that this might mean a considerable disruption in my lifestyle.

It was one of those life-changing decisions we all face from time to time. A door opens unexpectedly, a new direction offers itself, and we have the freedom to choose: to walk into the unknown or remain where we are. For me, it would have been easy and comfortable to simply stay put.

It was 1996, and I was living amid flowering trees and tropical gardens in the hinterland of Byron Bay on the northeastern coast of New South Wales, Australia. The house I called home was set on a ridge high above a pleasant landscape of rolling green fields. From every room, there was a view of the Pacific Ocean. In the distance, one could see our small beach town with its famous lighthouse, Australia's most easterly point.

This was my perfect paradise. Born and raised in a small town in Northern Germany, famous for its year-round cold, windy, and wet climate, I had moved to Berlin to study English, German, and Philosophy with the hope of becoming a writer. There, I cherished my newfound creative self-expression by contributing articles to feminist magazines and publishing my own experiential poetry.

At the same time, I felt restricted by a range of conventional ideas and expectations, assimilated since childhood, about who I should become and what I should be doing with my life. My father worked as a small claims court administrator, my mother was a passionate stay-at-home mom, and their dearest wish was that I become a high school teacher, and if not that, then at least a librarian. And so, at 25, my longing for freedom, adventure, and warmer weather pulled me out of Germany and sent me flying across the globe to Australia.

As the sun rose on my first morning in Sydney, I heard raucous, laughter-like sounds coming from the garden. I stumbled outside, and there sat a plump brown and white bird of about 16 inches with a huge beak laughing its head off: a kookaburra. Laughter is its song. Instantly, my love for this new country was born.

Australia fired up my creativity, drive, and ambition. In Sydney, I founded, developed, and eventually sold a domestic cleaning agency. I sat exams to become accredited as a translator and interpreter between English and German. After taking courses in accounting and working as a bookkeeper in Sydney for several years, I moved to the Byron Bay area and started offering bookkeeping services and accounting software training to small businesses.

From the local carpet shop to the doctor's office, from the finest restaurant in town to the little clothing store, my clients came from all walks of commercial life. Teaching them how to maintain bookkeeping on their computers and achieve a better understanding of their day-to-day financial reality was a fulfilling vocation.

But it didn't stop there. After a while, I realized that not only did I initiate my clients into the secrets of accounting software, but also, covertly, I was sharing deeper values, focusing more on taking back their power, becoming more self-reliant, and being in charge of their own lives. Passing on these precious gifts came naturally to me, and I began to understand that this had more to do with sharing myself than teaching actual techniques.

Self-employment suited me, and my self-esteem and confidence grew. Building a business, rising to the challenges of entrepreneurship, and enjoying the success that came my way—I embraced it all as confirmation that I was living the best possible life in the best place on the planet. I was sharp-minded and good-looking with a gorgeous body and firmly believed I could do anything.

Of course, it wasn't all fun and games. There were downsides. When a creature called "Success" arrived at my doorstep, it introduced me to its faithful companion, who went by the name of "Stress." Overwhelmed by my ever-growing workload and the responsibilities that went with it, I would go to bed thinking about the day's problems and would often be too busy to spend quality time with my friends.

My back was constantly sore, the result of chronically poor posture, hunched for hours over desks and computers. But I was somehow managing to nurse it with the help of regular bodywork, yoga, and swimming. Meditation practice, which I had started in my late teens, helped me stay psychologically healthy and clear.

During this time, I also suffered my share of heartbreak. Soon after arriving in Australia, I fell headlong in love with a man who, I was convinced, was the love of my life, but who, over time, proved otherwise. After five years of deep intimacy, we parted ways, and inevitably, I had to pass through a dark tunnel of sorrow and pain before I was able to stand once more in the healing light of the sun, face the world with a smile, and get on with my life.

A couple of years later, in Byron Bay, I entered into a new relationship. Still, after only twelve months, our connection, which at first had held so much promise for a fulfilling and long-term commitment – including talks of starting a family—was unravelling.

Watsu came into my life during this time. A few months after reading Harold Dull's book, I learned he was offering a two-week training in his Watsu method in Hawaii. I was immediately drawn to participate.

My boyfriend didn't want me to go since we were seeing a counsellor by that time, holding onto the last remaining thread of hope that things would work out. But for me, there was no question about attending the course. The pull was too strong. I had to go.

"See you soon," I whispered in our goodbye hug, but he said nothing. We both knew this was the end of our relationship.

I flew to Hawaii and joined Harold, his wife, his team, and a group of about twelve other participants on the Big Island at a small retreat center in the wilderness. A short drive away was a renowned black sand beach fringed by palm trees, where a lava flow from Kilauea, the island's most active volcano, had created a natural pool right next to the ocean. Pleasantly warm spring water flowed up from the bottom of the rocky pool. The Warm Pond, as it was known, was the most sensual place I could imagine and the ideal setting for Watsu.

My first Watsu session, given to me by one of Harold's assistants, was everything I had hoped it would be. There were moments when I could feel the vibration of pure lifeforce energy in every cell of my body, pulsing with a sensation of deep silence and oneness with all things. The training was off to a perfect start.

Every morning, we would learn and practice new Watsu moves at the Warm Pond, giving and receiving sessions. There was only a thin layer of rock between the pond and the ocean, so now and then, a refreshing surge of cold ocean water would splash over us.

Sadly, this exquisite spot no longer exists, as it was covered by a new lava flow caused by a big eruption from Kilauea several years later. But at the time, it was one of nature's miraculous gifts to anyone who knew about it.

Two weeks later, I somehow managed to return to Byron Bay and continue with my consulting business, which wasn't that easy, even though I loved my work. Who wants to go back to the office after being transported to paradise?

I settled into a new routine, continuing with my accounting and computer consulting business while making time to offer Watsu sessions in my own pool. Giving these sessions had an immediate impact on my state of well-being. Not only did I love every minute of it, but my back was also no longer hurting, and my mind and body had settled into a healthy balance.

I was beginning to understand my attraction to Watsu from a new perspective. It was helping me open up to my femininity, which I had neglected for years, preoccupied with my chosen role as the super-efficient entrepreneur. That was why an ecstatic shiver had passed through my body when I watched that first video, the invitation to utterly relax, surrender, and be moved through the yielding medium of warm water.

This balance of male and female energies, present in both men and women, was a concept I had learned as part of my interest in Tantra, the India-born art of exploring and transforming different kinds of human energy, including sexual, emotional, mental, and spiritual. In short, male energy is about doing and achieving, while female energy is about relaxing and receiving. To be given a Watsu session was my inner woman's idea of heaven.

Not to be outdone, my inner man also got involved because the natural next step was to teach Watsu, which appealed to "his" need for action, creating an ideal balance between the two sides of my male/female energy polarity. Moreover, I could see this form of bodywork becoming increasingly popular internationally in spa settings and physical therapy, and I could feel the excitement of being at the leading edge of a new wave.

Teaching required more training with Harold, which he offered at Harbin Hot Springs, a retreat center in Northern California where he lived and worked. Harold accepted me as an assistant in his Watsu classes.

My Australian friends were intrigued by my choice of repeatedly abandoning "normal" life in Byron Bay to chase Watsu dreams in exotic places around the planet.

But this is how change happens in life, isn't it? We move somewhere, settle into the new place, and make friends. A mini-world, a mini-society, is created around us without any special intention on our part. We think we know each other and can rely on each other. Daily life seems predictable and orderly, and suddenly a strong gust of change blows through, scattering all the pieces on the chessboard.

An acquaintance picked me up at San Francisco Airport. It was getting dark as we drove over the Golden Gate Bridge and headed north for two hours, passing over the Mayacamas mountain range at Mount Saint Helena and leaving the main highways behind for some narrow roads, winding up and down, left and right, through thick, dark forest.

It was a scary drive. In my daze of jet lag, I was getting nervous and thinking, "Gee, where are we going? We're heading deep into the backwoods! Why did I ever leave Australia for this strange experience?"

The pools at Harbin Hot Springs made up for it. They were spectacularly beautiful, surrounded by bay, oak, and fir trees set amongst scattered manzanita bushes with their distinctive reddish-brown branches. In the warm September sunshine, the heady fragrance in the air—combined with the warm temperature—made for a sensual environment. There was a large warm pool heated to body temperature, with a hot pool at one end and beyond that, a cold plunge and a large sun deck.

Very quickly, my favorite place became a specific spot in the warm pool where a spout brought the hot water in, massaging my back and sending shivers up and down my spine. I would half stand, half float. Above me was nothing but the blue sky and a magnificent fig tree, its branches bent heavy with fruit.

I swear, in my imagination, I could just open my mouth, and by the grace of God, a ripe fig might fall right into it. And I would slowly chew it and suck on it, letting its juices explode on my tongue, the ultimate sensual experience.

The first meeting of the Watsu class I was scheduled to assist began with introductions and logistics on Sunday evening in a conference room rather than in the pool. There were two more assistants, a warm-hearted, friendly guy called Daniel, and an invisible "Steve Carter" who seemed important. Supposedly he lived near Harbin but hadn't shown up.

The next morning at six o'clock, about 20 of us were in the pool, ready for our first water class. Up to my chest in warm water, I moved here and there, quietly helping the students, adjusting stances and arm positions. At one point, I was standing sideways next to a student giving a practice session. The person receiving was floating effortlessly on the water's surface, his head safely resting in the crook of the student's left arm and the back of his knees supported by her other arm.

"Raise your elbow a little and press more on the far shoulder," I encouraged the student softly. "Now, as you breathe in, feel the body rise, and as you breathe out, allow it to sink down gently. Enter into a slow rhythm with the breath. It'll create a subtle feeling of union between you and your client. Let your body rise and sink, too."

I was adjusting her elbow one more time when suddenly I heard a male voice near my right ear.

CHAPTER 2

THE LOVERS MEET

"Nope, that's not how you do it."

The intrusive remark came from behind.

Frowning, I glanced over my shoulder to see a confident-looking man, about 50 years old with strikingly clear blue eyes, zeroing in on me.

"Who are you to tell me what to do?" The words flew out of my mouth before I could stop them. I was an assistant to the main teacher. I knew my stuff. Who was this guy?

Before either of us could say more, Daniel, the other assistant, spotted the burgeoning conflict and came over.

"Steve, this is Lokita. She's the assistant from Australia."

The man called Steve blushed and backed off. Miffed and unsettled, I continued as best I could with the task of calmly supervising the session.

Later that morning, as I walked into the conference center where the classes on land were taking place, Steve approached me.

"I'm really so sorry," he told me, seemingly with genuine remorse. "I didn't realize you were an assistant."

I looked at him, taking my time to get the complete picture. He was a handsome man with bright eyes, thick and slightly wavy grey-silver hair, tanned smooth skin, and toned muscles. On top of it all, he looked so authentically sorry that I couldn't be offended any longer.

In fact, I felt attracted to this stranger. Unbidden by my rational mind, my heart beat faster, and butterflies danced in my stomach. Without rhyme or reason, I knew my life would never be the same.

I smiled and said, "Well, thank you. And by the way, it's all your fault."

When I was a girl, my mother had often warned me to think before I spoke, but now this odd sentence just floated out of my mouth, uncensored. Without further comment, we went into the classroom for the next session.

Steve introduced himself to the group, apologized for arriving late, and added, "I'm a Watsu teacher and massage therapist here at Harbin Hot Springs and one of your assistants for these two weeks."

For the entire morning, I was keenly aware of Steve's presence—where he was in the room, what he was doing, and who he was talking to—finding him more and more attractive.

Later, after we finished lunch and I was leaving the room to go back to my tent for a nap, Steve came up to me.

"Would you like to go for a walk?" he asked.

"Sure," I answered.

In the sweltering midday Californian heat, we went for a stroll among the trees and shrubs beyond the conference center, walking along a bubbling creek. He was in a pair of shorts, and I wore my bikini.

It was late summer, and Harbin was at its best. The sweet, heavy fragrance given off by the leaves of bay trees filled the air, so it was like wandering through a warm, perfumed garden. Just moving through this landscape was a sensual experience, mirroring the feeling of desire stirring inside me.

We chatted about this and that, and then, out of the blue, he paused, looked at me softly, and said, "Would you like to kiss?"

I nodded. I could hardly breathe. Awkwardly, we came close to each other. Our noses collided. Our lips seemed incompatible and we stopped, laughing at our clumsiness. Still, we had no intention of moving away from each other. The chemistry was there, even growing in intensity.

"Shall we try again?" This time it worked wonderfully. That's how we met. That's when we fell in love. The combination of laughter and desire was powerful and irresistible.

Soon it was time for the next Watsu class. Slowly, we made our way back.

"Why did you say it was my fault?" Steve wanted to know.

I took a deep breath. "Because my life is never going to be the same."

"Why?" he persisted.

"I just know it." I blushed under my tan, wondering if this time I had found "the one" I had been seeking all these years. Who knew whether he was even single? But because he kissed me, I presumed he was, which he later confirmed.

Before returning to class, we talked about ethics. We both knew it was inappropriate, indeed forbidden, to start a romance between two assistants in a Watsu course because it would be a distraction for everyone involved in the class.

Making love was out, but for the rest of the two-week training, we had fun secretly flirting with each other, sometimes with looks and smiles, sometimes taking time out for a clandestine kiss or two. We exchanged many Watsu sessions, getting to know each other in the space of silence, enjoying our growing intimacy.

Finally, the training was over. By then, we were more than ready to go deeper with each other and decided on a long weekend camping adventure.

I threw my bags into Steve's old blue Nissan pickup truck, and we drove north into the remote backcountry of Mendocino National Forest to the secret Crabtree Hot Springs. It was an isolated spot, far away in the mountains, with a cluster of four natural hot springs in a narrow, steep-walled canyon on the north bank of a river.

There, in our cozy tent, we made love for the first time, witnessed only by the animals of the night who rustled around us in the bushes. We transformed into two divine beings merging into the ultimate union of man and woman. We were perfectly matched in timing, intensity, and desire. Together we rode the waves of pleasure until we were spent, sweetly curling up in each other's arms to rest.

We spent several days in paradise—bathing in the hot springs, making love, cooking our food in nature, and rinsing our dishes in the flowing creek. California has many wild, isolated places that few people ever visit, and Crabtree Hot Springs is one of them.

After the camping trip, Harold phoned me. "Look, I know you've got a thing going on with Steve, and I know Steve's going to assist Margot Anand in a workshop in Hawaii that I'm teaching with her in a couple of weeks, so how'd you like to come along as my assistant?"

"Yes...yes...yes...oh yes!" Well, I probably didn't say it quite like that to Harold, but that's how I felt, almost jumping out of my skin with excitement, and he got the message.

I knew Margot Anand as the charismatic French woman who had written the first and best-selling Western Tantra manual, *The Art of Sexual Ecstasy*, which played a seminal role in the introduction and expansion of Tantra in both Europe and the US during the 1990s.

I had attended her workshops and trainings and was intrigued by this ancient Indian art of ecstatic lovemaking and spiritually oriented intimacy. Tantra offered a way to enjoy a more fulfilled life by integrating meditation into everyday activities. Over the years, I had studied Tantra with other teachers, but Margot's way suited me best. I knew Steve had also trained extensively with Margot and was close friends with her.

I was excited about being part of this workshop because it combined everything I loved: Hawaii, Watsu, Tantra, and, last but not least, my new lover. It would be easy for me to go to Hawaii. All I had to do was change my return flight to Australia and advise my customers. But how would Steve feel about it?

"Have you told Steve?" I asked Harold.

"No, I'll leave that up to you."

That same evening, Steve and I had a dinner date. "I spoke to Harold today," I ventured, carefully choosing my words. "He suggested I join him, Margot, and you in Hawaii for the Watsu and Tantra workshop."

Steve looked at me and began tapping his fingers on the tabletop. His lips pressed together in one long line before he spoke.

"Oh, I don't know, Lokita! I'm not sure about this. Maybe it's too much, too soon!"

"Hmm, maybe you're right." I appeared to agree, but inwardly I felt just the opposite. Of course, he wasn't right!

"But hey, life is short, so why not? Come on, we'll just go to Hawaii for a week, have some fun, and figure it out as we go along," I suggested. "It'll be lovely, and if it turns out not to be...well, I'm going back to Australia anyway."

He agreed. By now, we were headlong in love, and the unexpected week in Hawaii would give us a chance to get to know each other better and discover whether this was a passing affair or the beginning of a long-term love story.

Off we went to Hawaii. The workshop was held at a luxury resort, whereas we, the assistants, were accommodated at the small Bamboo Hut lodge next door. Our room was boring and the opposite of romantic.

"We definitely need to do something about this," Steve raised his eyebrows, looking around the bare-bones room. "I have an idea. Let's transform it into a love nest!"

Since we were the only guests in the lodge, we visited all the other bedrooms, picking out plants, decorations, and furniture. We carried it all back to ours and set up our sacred love space. The owners laughed and didn't object.

Harold and Margot arrived a couple of days later, and their workshop began. The balmy, tropical environment, the warm waters, and the powerful tantric practices allowed us to open our hearts, let go, and dive deep into the experience of being alive.

During the week, Margot and Harold invited us to demonstrate and lead some of the workshop sessions, and to our delight, Steve and I discovered that we very much enjoyed teaching together. The magical key was that we were already immersed in the experience of love and intimacy that we were sharing with the group. We didn't just teach Tantra; we *were* Tantra. We radiated Tantra.

In essence, Tantra is embodied spirituality, embracing the body as a gateway to higher consciousness. The teachings of Tantra include sexuality, which has led the media to write about it with sensational headlines, such as reports of seven-hour orgasms and all-night orgies. Yet there is much more to it. It is a way of life.

As *Tantrikas*, we know that when sexual energy is moved consciously up the spine, it becomes spiritual ecstasy. At the highest moment of lovemaking, two lovers become one, and everything else melts away. We can access the divine within ourselves and with our partner by breathing together, communicating consciously, and making love with deep acceptance of what is happening, here and now in the present moment. Whether things are easy or difficult, everything in life is welcomed as a learning process.

Steve's and my teaching style emerged right then and there: uncompromising authenticity, offering only what we had experienced and embodied. Later, we were lauded for "walking our talk" because Tantra can only be shared by those who understand the meaning of the exercises and know how to practice them. It's not an intellectual route to enlightenment and outstanding sex.

The workshop was a success. Harold, Margot, and the 30 or so participants loved our presentations, and although we didn't realize it at the time, our teaching partnership was born.

Then came the truly hard part: I had to return to Australia.

It was our final night in our Bamboo Hut love nest. We had just made love and were lying close together. The crickets were chirping, the fragrance of night jasmine wafted through the air, and countless stars sprinkled the dark blue night sky with a confetti of fairy lights. Turning to me, Steve kissed my nose and murmured, "Well, if you want to come back to California and be with me, you're welcome. I'll even marry you."

That blew my mind. Steve had been married before and had two children, so this was a huge step for him.

With a quivering voice, I breathed, "Yes, I'd love to marry you!"

My legs were shaking all the way back to San Francisco, where we parted ways, Steve to return to his home near Harbin and me to board a plane for Australia.

We had planned to meet again in a few months, but by the time I walked into my office in Byron Bay, I had the feeling it would be only a few weeks. Love had touched my heart and asked me to assess the true value of the lifestyle I had set up for myself in Australia. When we die, we cannot take anything with us but the quality, the taste, and the feeling of love.

It happened really fast. I gave away my business to the staff, packed up my belongings, moved out of my home, and bid farewell to my friends, many of whom were scratching their heads and wondering if I was being overly hasty—to put it mildly—in dropping everything and jetting off to the US to live with a newly found lover.

Change enters our lives again and again, and we are often afraid of it. Venturing into the unfamiliar, leaving everything behind, was scary.

Yet I knew one thing for sure. Trusting in true love is such a power that it gives us the wings to fly, the courage to let go of everything we possess, the confidence to throw caution to the wind, and go dancing and weightless into the unknown.

CHAPTER 3

A WORLD OF OUR OWN

"Look into each other's eyes," I breathed into the microphone, carefully watching the 26 participants in the room in front of me. They were in pairs, sitting on cushions on the floor, facing each other. Some were couples in long-term relationships, while others were single and had just met. Their ages ranged between 25 and 70. All of them were keen to experience Tantra.

"Keep looking at each other, allowing your gaze to be soft and relaxed," I instructed softly. "Now, in your own time, gently place your right hand on your partner's heart."

Regardless of age, gender, skin color, financial circumstances, or relationship status, the deep longing for love was the human quality that brought us all together. Hence, we found ourselves in very diverse company during our workshops. For example, we might have a young couple participating on a financial scholarship in the same room as a well-known billionaire and his wife. Or there would be a Hollywood celebrity doing practices with our local gardener from down the road.

"Cover your partner's hand with your left hand," I continued. "Notice that you're connected through your hands and your hearts…when you feel ready, close your eyes and feel the inner connection…heart to heart…."

As I clutched the microphone, the palms of my hands were clammy, and I could feel the tell-tale red blush on my neck. I tried my best to prevent nervousness from creeping into my voice, wishing to come across as loving, soft, and encouraging. This was the first Tantra workshop in which I equally shared the microphone with Steve.

Smiling, I gave him a sideways glance at his place beside me. He smiled back with encouragement. We could do this. We could offer Tantra workshops, fill them with eager clients, and guide them to those precious states of ecstasy and meditation we both knew were available to everyone. We felt like a dream team doing a dream job, and I could scarcely believe my good fortune.

It had been a huge gamble, an act of trust in the mystery of life, to come to California and live with Steve in his home just outside Harbin Hot Springs. We were overjoyed to be together again, but after driving the one hundred miles from San Francisco airport to Middletown, Steve admitted that he was nervous about me moving in with him.

"You can live in the downstairs apartment and pay me rent." His voice sounded formal. "I'll live upstairs, and we'll see each other when we want to."

"Okay, fine. Let's do that." I was jet-lagged, and this wasn't the time to question his boundaries. Besides, I hoped our new love could overcome whatever fears we had.

The arrangement didn't last long. Two weeks later, Steve invited me to live with him upstairs.

The downstairs apartment became our love temple, our sacred space. There were no neighbors close by, only magnificent nature outside. The living room would be flooded with golden sunlight coming through a floor-length window. We would lie on the thick rug, make love, tell each other our histories and hopes for the future, play with each other, giving and receiving pleasure, melting and merging until the sun moved across the sky and shadows fell on us. Then we would drag the rug across the floor, back into the sunlight, and make love some more. We would talk, laugh, roll around, and eat our meals on that rug. We were on the magic carpet ride that all new lovers know.

One afternoon, Steve told me about his idea of leading a Tantra seminar together. For some time, it had been his dream to find a beloved with whom he could create a teaching partnership, and I was one hundred percent on board.

Soon, we were planning our first workshop, which we called "Timeless Loving." We would show participants how to tap into the flow of energy within themselves and with others. We would encourage them to connect with their hearts and feelings, opening themselves outwardly to love and moving inwardly into meditation, where time and space disappear.

They would receive practices they could take into their daily lives and explore for themselves in their own private, intimate setting.

Explicit sexual activity wouldn't be part of our teaching, nor would orgies or other exotic activities that the media commonly associate with the word "Tantra."

We made a proposal to the Harbin Hot Springs workshops department, which was in charge of programming and renting out their conference facilities. Until then, they had been hesitant to include Tantra workshops in their offerings, fearing the possibility of sleaze and scandal, but they had known Steve for many years as a man of integrity and common sense, so they gave us a chance.

The first workshop went well, and although it may have looked effortless to the participants, it was hard work for us. To make sure our clients got good value, we packed the program with so many practices for enhancing intimacy, awakening sexual energy, and deepening love that by the end, everybody was completely exhausted but with big smiles on their faces. Many participants returned for more of our workshops and remained good friends over the following years.

Fundamentally, aside from the training and support we received from our teacher Margot Anand, the success of our professional partnership stemmed from our unwavering commitment to our love, to Tantra as our spiritual path, and to inspiring others to broaden their horizons. Over time, Steve and I morphed into what we called "one thing" – the two of us together became one. Often, we would lovingly remind each other that we were "one thing," and this always brought us closer together, whether we had just made love or had an argument.

As individuals, we had a perfect balance. Steve was a flowing person who could easily embrace new situations, whereas I was more structured, preferring to rely on plans and strategies.

In this respect, I have always been a true German. I appreciated how, in Germany, things get done on time, society is disciplined and organized, and systems work smoothly. It could be quite challenging for me to deal with spontaneous, unplanned situations, whereas for Steve, it was quite the opposite.

I remember one occasion a few years later, when we were in the habit of taking long vacation breaks in Costa Rica, Steve impulsively decided to buy "Rojito," a bright red, tiny old Datsun lowrider pickup truck. There were several pressing issues to deal with, including badly needed repairs, registration, and insurance.

A man on a mission, Steve drove off to Cóbano, the nearest big town, with no appointments, no idea with whom he should talk, nor how to handle the logistics of car ownership in this country.

"Sure," I thought to myself, anticipating the difficulties he would encounter as I watched him disappear down the road from where we were staying. "Let's see how he's going to achieve all that!"

I couldn't believe my eyes when he returned a few hours later with everything taken care of.

"How on earth did you manage it?"

Laughingly, Steve told me his story. Driving into Cóbano, he felt thirsty, so he stopped at a store and bought drinking water. He chatted up the charming, attractive cashier, who told him about her friend, a mechanic just around the corner. She called him, and he happened to have free time right then. And luckily, across the road from him was a car part store that stocked the necessary parts.

Talking to the mechanic in his very own version of Spanish with lots of sign language— gesticulating wildly with hands and feet— Steve found out that by chance, the mechanic's brother, living a few houses down the road, was the local car insurance agent. He also knew a lawyer to whom Steve could go for car registration papers, who was a cousin of his wife.

Her office was behind the insurance agent's house, and she was available for a consultation. Steve was riding the current wherever it took him and achieved what, to me, had been inconceivable. I was flabbergasted.

Episodes like this encouraged both of us, especially me, to relax more and more into the waves of life, to surrender fixed ideas, and become open to the possibilities that exist everywhere, in every moment. Our lives were an ongoing dance of yin and yang, feminine and masculine, relaxation and effort, control and surrender in our relationship, in day-to-day activities, and in our intimate practices and meditations.

Like any couple, we faced challenges in our exploration of being together. The desire to melt and merge is strong when lovers first meet, yet some qualities make us unique as individuals, make Steve "Steve" and me "Lokita." We may find some of these character traits challenging, even infuriating, but we cannot change our partner. On the contrary, we need to love and respect each other for who we are.

For example, although we were committed to being monogamous, Steve and I both liked to flirt. We were charismatic, vibrant, good-looking people with nice bodies who enjoyed connecting with people.

Flirting, for me, means being open, playfully communicating and relating, sometimes with a little innuendo of sexiness, sometimes with just fun and sweetness, but always with an open heart and a willingness to make genuine contact.

Flirting does not mean that I wish to have a sexual experience or emotional attachment with somebody. But neither does being in a monogamous relationship mean that all other doors have to close and all other people, especially men, are excluded from my life.

Steve enjoyed the feeling of being admired and wanted by others. But there was a classic problem because although he liked to flirt, he didn't like me doing the same.

He didn't say anything, but I could tell when he was jealous and feeling threatened. There came a time early in our relationship when I felt the need to sit down with him and talk about it.

"Look, Steve, we're both attractive," I began. "We've decided to be monogamous, but I'm a flirtatious person. I like to laugh. I like to be playful with men...."

Steve sat there, looking at me with a long, stoic face.

"Basically, that's who I am," I explained. "There are certain traits that make up my personality, and this is one of them. It's also part of what you find attractive in me, so this is the package you get.

"I've been like this since long before I met you, and if you don't like that part of me, that's too bad because I'm going to be like this to my very end, even when I'm 97 years old," I continued.

"To stop flirting would be like cutting off a major part of who I am," I added. "I like to relate to men, but it doesn't mean there's a desire to be sexual with them. There's no threat to our relationship, and I want you to know that."

Steve made a wry face, grimacing a little and chewing his lower lip. Then he took a deep breath and managed a lopsided smile.

"Well, I don't really like it, but I see your point."

As a couple, we were well-matched in that way. We had the capacity to listen to each other. We had the courage to look at ourselves through the other person's eyes and acknowledge what was being seen.

We could also embrace new perspectives for ourselves and grow, so much so that one day my heart skipped a beat when Steve told me, "You know, I do enjoy watching you receive attention from other men and exercising your 'flirt muscle.' You're very sexy, and I'm so proud that you're my woman!" We both laughed.

On March 10th, 1999, four months after my arrival in California, we dressed in our smartest clothes and left home in great excitement. We had decided to get married at the local courthouse in Clearlake, located approximately 20 minutes from our home.

However, after a few miles of driving, Steve's mood changed, and the atmosphere in the pickup truck's cab grew serious and tense. A major thunderstorm was brewing inside our car. Eventually, he pulled over, stopped the truck, and lowered his head on the steering wheel, hugging it with his arms.

"I'm sorry, Lokita. I don't think I can go through with this," he murmured. "I'm afraid it's not going to work out between us."

He turned to look at me, his eyes moist. "I'm worried that you will leave me. I'm worried that my family won't like you." He took a deep breath and looked at me. "And I'm worried that maybe I'm just too difficult for you."

His confession shocked me. I didn't know what to say. Facing the possibility that we might not get married, I sat still, listening to Steve's long list of fears.

As he started driving again, I stared out the window, holding on to the door handle and watching the landscape fly past as if in a strange dream.

By the time we arrived in the courthouse parking lot, we were overwhelmed and exhausted by the doubts and angst that had been swirling around inside the car.

Steve turned off the ignition, and suddenly it was eerily still in the cab. As we stepped out on either side of the truck, I looked across the cab's roof. There was Steve, the man of my dreams, his shoulders hanging, his face pale, and the corners of his mouth turned downwards.

I took a deep breath. "My love, this is supposed to be the happiest day of our lives." I paused. "But if it's a miserable day for you, perhaps it'd be best if we didn't get married."

Our gazes met with electrifying intensity. One could cut the air with a knife. I was one hundred percent prepared for whatever would come next.

It seemed like an eon as we stared at each other in silence. Suddenly, Steve burst out laughing. Whoosh! That was it. All his doubts and fears evaporated. All his history of pain with relationships vanished. We connected, here and now, in the present moment, in trust and love.

We didn't know how our love affair would work out, but we weren't going to let any baggage from the past rule us. We simply surrendered to the moment and said, "Yes! Let's do this!"

By the time we made it into the courthouse chamber, it was closing time, and the chairs were already up on the tables for floor cleaning. Even so, a wise and patient judge and his secretary welcomed us for our wedding ceremony. The setting was rather unromantic, yet as the judge recited the vows we were about to make to each other, we locked eyes. We both knew that in this private, powerful moment, outside circumstances were irrelevant. This ceremony was about Steve and me. Nothing else mattered.

Later that year, after we had gone public with our marriage, we had two more wedding celebrations—one in June at Harbin Hot Springs surrounded by the community and another in October when our families and friends all came together, officiated by one of Steve's oldest friends. I walked down the aisle on my father's arm, wrapped in a slinky, light purple satin wedding gown, draped by a veil my mother had sewn and adorned with countless tiny pearls.

A year after our wedding, Costa Rica entered our lives. We had been invited to hold a workshop at a picturesque mountaintop resort boasting spectacular views. It was close to the country's main international airport and an ideal location. At night the sea of city lights glittered below us, and we could watch the New Year's fireworks from above. It was magical.

Our participants, mainly from the US, enjoyed the exotic atmosphere and tropical climate, happy to leave the cold North American winter behind them.

It was such a success that we were invited back year after year. After our second retreat, we discovered Montezuma, a little beach town in the southernmost part of the Nicoya Peninsula on the Pacific Ocean. It was a gorgeous place, and from then on, we went back every winter.

One morning in 2005, while we were in Montezuma, we walked up a nearby steep hill. The air was steamy with heat and humidity, and our skin dripped with sweat.

"Steve, can we stop here for a minute?" I needed to catch my breath. Turning off to the right was a narrow, gravelly side road leading into a maze of tropical foliage.

"Let's walk up there and then take a break," Steve said. "I wonder what we'll find!"

Before long, we sat in the shade of a huge old tree, cooling down, our legs stretched out toward a spectacular ocean view. Below us, as far as the eyes could see, there was nothing but the vibrating green wildness of the rainforest and beyond it the vast expanse of blue ocean. Just then, a group of pelicans flew by below us. All we could hear were parrots screeching somewhere in the distance. Tiny white fishing *pangas* floated along the horizon.

Suddenly, out of nowhere, the sound of an arriving car startled us out of our reverie. I turned around. Steve jumped to his feet.

A Costa Rican man got out of the car, looking at us, his eyebrows raised in a questioning manner.

"Buenos días. What are you doing here? Que pasa?"

Steve was apologetic. "Oh, perdón. We didn't mean to trespass, but it's such a lovely spot. Do you know anything about it? Maybe it's for sale?"

Immediately, the man's expression turned into a broad smile.

"Si, claro, it's for sale, and I'm the owner."

"Fantástico. How much is it?" Steve and I had thought vaguely before then about buying property in Costa Rica.

He mentioned a figure, and our hearts leaped. With a bank loan, we could afford to buy it, and so the Costa Rican dream began.

We started developing the grounds. As a first step, we hired a young man named Bladimir to care for the property in our absence. He proved trustworthy and skilled with plants and is still my gardener today.

After several years preparing the land, in 2011, we built a one-bedroom house with a large high-ceilinged living room, a covered patio, a bathroom, an open-plan kitchen, and a small office, all with spectacular ocean views.

In December of that year, we moved in. On our first morning, nature presented us with an unusual gift. The growling sounds of the howler monkeys in the distance awakened me, and I could see through my half-opened eyes that the sun was just rising, casting a golden light across the ocean. Even though I was sleepy, I stumbled onto the patio to welcome this new day, the first in our new home.

As I opened the glass sliding door, I looked down. There was a strange brown pile of something indefinable right by the door. It looked slimy and measured some 30 inches in diameter.

"Aargh! What is that? Looks like a very large piece of poop!" I went back into the room to get my flip-flops and glasses.

And then I saw what it was: a huge boa constrictor curled up right outside our new bedroom door.

What a sight! She must have been about 30 feet long. Well, okay, maybe 15 feet, but that's still a very big snake! I guessed she had been living in this neighborhood for many years. Somehow, she belonged in our garden.

I took her presence as a good omen. In Eastern spiritual traditions, snakes hold strong symbolic value as signs of good luck, fertility and creation, transformation and rebirth. In Tantric traditions, a snake symbolizes divine feminine energy.

After watching her for a while, I gingerly stepped back inside the bedroom, closed the sliding door, and then, embracing the boa constrictor's energy, I slithered snake-like under the sheets and made love in a deliciously serpentine way with Steve. An excellent way to bless our new bed!

Everything about our house was fresh, virgin, waiting to be explored and integrated into our lives. In fact, some parts of the house weren't even ready when we moved in. For example, there was no mirror in the bathroom. The large one we had chosen had not arrived yet.

Everything else was there. We would brush our teeth over the sink, raise our heads, and look at a blank wall where we would never see ourselves.

This is how we discovered another intimate way of relating: by using each other as mirrors. Relationships, in general, hold up the mirror in front of us, and in the reflection, we can see much about ourselves that was invisible before.

Living without a physical mirror was liberating because one typically spends quite a bit of time examining oneself, adjusting this and that. For Steve and me, it became completely normal to be without one.

Gradually, we realized that we wanted to spend more and more time in Costa Rica, and for Steve, this transition included a four-legged addition to our family.

"I'd like to get a dog," he confided one day as we glanced out over the ocean. "A big dog with short hair, a guard dog, like a Doberman."

"What? A Doberman? Are you joking? That's the most dangerous dog I can imagine!"

The only Doberman I knew was the notoriously fierce "Diablo," uncrowned king of all dogs in Montezuma, and I couldn't imagine having a "pet" like him in my life.

Steve persisted, so when we returned to California, he found a breeder who had a litter of four puppies, only a few weeks old. The smallest one looked up at Steve with her big, golden, innocent eyes. He smiled. It was love at first sight.

In March 2012, two-month-old baby "Coco" came into our lives, named by us because of the color of her hair. Theoretically, she was *our* Doberman, but Steve adored Coco so much that they quickly became inseparable.

I took on the role of mother, the one who fed the dog, cleaned up after her, washed her, and took care of medical stuff like vaccinations. In this way, she became my *doghter*. But Steve was the man with the dog, taking her for long walks, playing games with her, and training her.

In mid-2013, after Steve's father had passed away, we began talking about a permanent shift to Montezuma, but we soon discovered we had different ideas about our future, which created challenges.

I was 50 years old; Steve was 65. I saw the move as "business as usual," and he saw it as retirement. I still wanted to teach and travel; he wanted to cut down the number of workshops, spend more quality time with me, go surfing, practice yoga, chill out with local friends, play with the dog, and enjoy life away from work. His priorities in life had shifted, whereas mine had not.

It was the first time our age difference became an issue because I wasn't ready to retire. At the time, we were at the height of our professional success. During the past fourteen years, we had led over five hundred workshops and trainings, teaching thousands of people across the US, on Caribbean cruises, in Canada, Bermuda, Costa Rica, and Mexico. We were, as one newspaper article put it, "the most consistently successful Tantra workshop leaders in America."

Teaching on the cruises was always a special treat. Apart from our well-frequented events that attracted hundreds of people on the boat, just being on a cruise liner was so much fun. Steve loved getting dressed up for the costume parties or the fine dinner at the captain's table. He especially liked the formal nights when he would don his tuxedo and strut around proudly with his red bowtie and cummerbund. We would pose together for photographs, me in a sleek evening gown with my dashing husband by my side, all elegance and style.

Our events would take place while at sea. On shore days, we would visit exotic islands and go on excursions and adventures. Steve would marvel wide-eyed at everything we encountered, be it scuba-diving in Bonaire, the fish market in Petit-Bourg, Guadeloupe, or meeting a woman from Munich in a café on the island of Martinique who had the same birthday as him. He would constantly talk with the locals, and although he might not have spoken their native tongue, his exuberant, enthusiastic voice helped everyone understand exactly what he was trying to say.

It was the same with his Spanish. In Costa Rica, he would talk especially loudly with his hands and smile; people loved him for it. When he went shopping, he always came home with the right things.

Now Steve wanted to lie back in a hammock and chill out while I felt we were on a roll and could expand even more. I loved meeting new people, sharing our Tantra vision with them, and watching their lives become richer and happier.

The divergence between us started in the late Spring of 2013 and went on well into the middle of 2014. It wasn't an easy year. We hit some major roadblocks, and after many time-outs and conversations, we reached an agreement. It wasn't so much a negotiation that got us there as finding a common denominator, which was one of the Tantric tools we taught in our workshops.

Steve wanted to move to Costa Rica and retire. I also wanted to live in Costa Rica but not always stay there. So, we found common ground on the location but not on the length of time we would spend there.

We agreed that we would move to Montezuma, live there for two years, and teach a few workshops in the US and Costa Rica. Only then would we compare notes to see if we both liked it enough to make a long-term and full-time commitment to our new home and lifestyle.

We were both pleased with what we decided. But still, it was a gut-wrenching experience for me because shifting to Costa Rica meant putting our California house up for sale and selling our workshop business.

I found myself grieving their loss. A true homebody, the house and grounds had been my refuge, and the business, my baby, had given me so much satisfaction. Establishing, managing, and expanding it had been my creative outpouring. My life had definition, purpose, and direction. Now I had to take a long, fresh look at who I was in the world and what I wanted to do. A vast empty space stretched out in front of me.

Nevertheless, by the time Steve and I were ready to move, I had worked through my hesitation, and we were both excited about what life would present us with in our new location. The dream of living in beautiful Costa Rica was becoming a reality.

We moved on December 8th, 2014, and despite what we had been through to get there, we were happy to be in our new home. The sun was shining on us, and the weather forecast for our relationship and our future was warm and calm. And as we gazed out together across the ocean of possibilities ahead of us, we were completely oblivious to the monstrous hurricane approaching.

CHAPTER 4

A SUSPICIOUS SPOT

"Mrs. Carter, I need to talk with you about a suspicious spot we have detected in your left breast."

A shiver of fear ran through me. The young woman in the white coat was pleasant enough, but she wasn't my usual radiologist, and I didn't feel the same comforting rapport with her as with her predecessor.

She seemed too young to be experienced in her field. Mind you, I was 51 years old by then, and to me, anyone under 40 looked too young to be a doctor.

It was October 2014, two months before our move to Costa Rica, and I had gone for my annual so-called "routine" mammogram at a breast care clinic in Santa Rosa, California.

It was never routine for me. My mother had died of breast cancer seven years earlier, and the possibility that the breast cancer gene had been passed from her to me was lurking like an ominous shadow in the back of my mind, ready to pounce at any moment. Even so, I decided against taking the gene test designed to predict the likelihood of developing breast cancer. Would I have my breasts amputated if the test was positive for the BRCA gene? Probably not.

So, although it was frightening, I preferred not to know. Knowing would somehow be scarier because I would have to make a choice.

Mutti had not told anybody that she was sick or that she suspected that she had cancer. My younger sister Wiebke, my father, and I only found out about it when she was in the hospital and diagnosed with stage IV breast cancer. That meant that the cancer had spread to other parts of her body and, in her case, was no longer treatable. After she died, her doctor told me that the size of her tumor and that it had broken through the skin meant that she must have been living with breast cancer for seven to ten years.

I had often pondered over my mother's decision not to talk about her condition. Was she in denial of her reality, or did she want to save us from knowing the hard truth? How would I handle it if I were diagnosed with cancer?

A year or so before she died, our family had gone on a bicycle trip one sunny Sunday afternoon. My father was the leader of our little peloton, followed by my sister and me, with my mother taking up the rear. After a thrilling ride across a long bridge with only a bare metal grid for a bottom, we came to a particularly complicated and dangerous intersection, with cars and trucks converging from several directions.

My father stopped, as did my sister and I, but Mutti continued at full speed, buoyed by the exhilaration of the bridge, sailing blithely through the intersection, laughing loudly, vibrant with freedom and love for life. She was a rebel then, a wild woman I hardly recognized. The mother I knew was usually placid and reserved and didn't tend to demonstrations of exuberance.

Later, after she died, the memory of my mother's carefree abandon on her bicycle returned to me again and again. She may not have wanted us to know about the cancer because she had wished to let her hair down and live fully until she died, knowing she had to make the most out of the limited time she had left. Somehow these thoughts helped me find peace with her not telling us.

After the mammogram, I was sitting outside the scanning room, dressed and ready to leave, when the technician who had been operating the mammography machine came through the door, hands in the pockets of her lab coat, and said, "Mrs. Carter, if you don't mind, we need to take a few more pictures."

This didn't sound good. It wasn't routine. With shaky legs, I followed the technician back into the scanning room and repeated the same procedure, this time with more X-rays and in different positions.

When it was over, I got dressed and returned to the waiting room. There was a hollow feeling in my stomach, and instinctively I wanted to run away.

That was when the radiologist told me about the suspicious spot. "We can't determine from the X-rays whether it's benign or malignant, so I recommend you have a core needle biopsy as soon as possible."

The ground below my feet fell away. Immediately, my mind seized on the worst-case scenario. "Oh no! This is it! Seven years since Mutti died, and now it's my turn. I knew it!"

In 2007, within a few months of my mother's death, I had been scheduled for my first mammogram, a stressful prospect for me. As a result, a boil had developed on my left breast, just below the nipple. My doctor had assured me that it wasn't anything to be worried about, but even for an apparently benign boil, it had taken several months to heal and left a small scar.

When the radiologist showed me an X-ray picture and pointed at the suspicious spot, I could see that it was exactly where the boil had been.

"We need a biopsy," she repeated emphatically.

My heart was pounding. To me, "biopsy" was a loaded word. I didn't consider it a positive term, culminating in an all-clear announcement that I was whole and healthy. Not at all. To me, it implied cancer and certain death.

"Okay, here's your appointment, Mrs. Carter." The nurse practitioner handed me a slip of paper.

"In this procedure, the doctor inserts a needle into your breast and takes out small samples of breast tissue to be analyzed by a pathologist," she explained. "It's very standard. Don't worry about it too much."

Don't worry? My heart had dropped down through the floor.

"We'll see you in two weeks then."

With that, I entered a new and scary territory.

During the drive home, my thoughts were on a repeating loop. "This is it. I have breast cancer. How am I going to get through this?"

Steve was working in the garden. He had so much enthusiasm for plants! In addition to a large field of kale, pumpkin, melon, and zucchini, we had an orchard overflowing with apples, traditional and Asian pears, plums, grapes, quince, persimmons, olives, Meyer lemons, and my all-time favorite—fat, juicy black Mission figs. The local grocery stores were happy to buy countless pounds of his produce every year. "Steve's Organics," it said on their labels, and people snapped them up.

If I were looking for Steve, most often I would find him in the garden, with a big smile on his face, his hands dirty, and Coco by his side. He also used the garden therapeutically. Whenever he was upset or something was bothering him, he would go into the garden and dig a hole. I could always judge from the size and depth of the hole how Steve was feeling.

"Hello, my love. How did it go?"

When I said nothing, he looked up from his shovel.

"Well…" My voice was wobbly. "There's a suspicious spot, and I've got to have a biopsy."

He scratched his head, then smiled, "Oh, it's probably nothing. Biopsies are usually just a way to make sure everything is alright."

In his eyes, I saw naked fear. He knew I was afraid of breast cancer, and now here it was, knocking on our door, just when we were looking forward to moving to Costa Rica, just when he was expecting life to get easier, more carefree, more like peaceful retirement.

The biopsy was performed at the same clinic by the same doctor. It had sounded easy enough. In truth, it was invasive and painful. My poor breast was bruised for days afterwards.

A week or so later, I got the biopsy results: benign, which meant I didn't have cancer. I ended the call with a bright smile and skipped into the garden to tell Steve.

His voice was jubilant, "You see? It was nothing." And for a short while, I felt the same.

But my relief was short-lived. One morning in the shower, about five weeks after the biopsy, I was soaping my body when I noticed a lump in my left breast, just below the skin, in the exact spot where the scar from my boil was located.

My heart sank and my fears rose. I looked down at my breast. I looked at it in the mirror. Nothing was visible from the outside, but I could feel a hard, tumor-like swelling about the size of a small almond.

A heavy blanket of dread settled on my shoulders. We were packed and ready for the flight to Costa Rica. Just then, Steve walked into the bathroom and I showed him my discovery.

"Should we put our plans on hold?" I asked. We looked at each other, silently weighing the options.

"Well, we could stay in California, at least until that strange lump has been diagnosed properly," Steve said. "But since it's so close to Christmas, I imagine we won't get a new appointment until early in the New Year."

I sighed. He was right. Besides, the new owners of our house were ready to move in, the cars were sold, furniture donated, and our remaining belongings were in a shipping container, far out to sea, on their way to Costa Rica. Trying to sound convincing, I said, "In any case, the biopsy was benign, so it's probably *really* nothing,"

"Or maybe just scar tissue from the biopsy," he ventured. We agreed that our departure should remain on schedule.

By the time we arrived in Costa Rica, the lump had grown to the size of a pecan, and constant pain had begun to radiate through the left side of my rib cage.

"What could it be?" I wondered. I felt confused because I had heard that breast cancer didn't hurt, whereas this lump definitely did.

In bed at night, I would lie on my belly with a pillow under my stomach and below my chest so that the breast could be free from pressure. That would alleviate the pain at first, but soon I could no longer sleep, and it became unbearable. Despite the benign biopsy results, I decided to see a doctor in San José.

It was a five-hour trip from our remote beach town to Costa Rica's capital city, including a drive, a ferry ride, and another drive. Alternatively, one could take a 20-minute flight in a light aircraft but bouncing around amid the cumulus clouds in a 12-seater propeller plane wasn't exactly my favorite method of transport. I chose the ground option.

Dr. Heraldo Botella was young, charismatic, and quite flirtatious. He had been recommended as an excellent breast surgeon, sounded convincing and knowledgeable, and charmed me with his friendly, confident manner.

The doctor gave me an ultrasound. "Por favor, don't worry, Lokita. Bueno, it's probably a hematoma inside the breast caused by the punch biopsy." He made a note on his writing pad and explained that a hematoma is a type of blood-filled bruise hidden beneath the skin. "Visit me again if it doesn't improve in the next month."

I returned to Montezuma. The problem didn't go away. By the time February rolled around, the lump, now the size of a walnut in its shell, had broken through the skin. Its surface was pink and light brown, smooth in places and scaly in others, reminiscent of a severe, blistery burn.

First thing each morning, I would look in the mirror. Filled with dread and fear, I would see that new ridges had appeared inside the breast and outside on the skin. It was getting urgent; my breast was aflame with a dull, agonizing pain. Something was not right.

On the internet, I studied images of different types of breast cancer and carefully monitored my breast for outward signs of what I thought was the worst type of all: inflammatory breast cancer. My breast didn't look like any of those pictures, so I was still hopeful that this growing lump had some other cause.

I went back to Dr. Heraldo in San José, and he assured me once again that it wasn't cancer. "It's probably a bacterial infection." He shrugged. "I think you should see a virologist to check for tropical diseases."

The virologist prescribed an ointment. It didn't help. As the months passed and the lump refused to disappear, I had several more biopsies in San José, overseen by Dr. Heraldo. They all came back benign, but the hurting, swelling, and growth continued.

One sunny morning in July, after Steve had gone to his yoga class, I was looking vacantly at the ocean view, feeling the pain pulsating in my breast, and I knew at that moment that something had to be done and done now. There and then, I decided to fly to San José immediately.

Despite my fear of small planes, I booked a flight, drove to the local airport, and flew to San José. By the time I was there, about an hour later, Steve had returned from yoga to an empty house.

He picked up on the first ring. "Hello, my love. I flew to San José to see the doctor."

"What? That's crazy!" If there had been any doubt in him, by now he began to realize how serious this was. Otherwise, I would never have volunteered to fly in a light aircraft.

"Steve, it's unbearable. It can't go on like this. There's something very wrong with my breast." My voice was getting shrill. "I have to do something *right now*."

"Okay, I totally understand. Call me as soon as you've talked to the doctor. I love you!"

Dr. Heraldo was charming as usual, although I have to say that, by this time, his flirtatious manner was wearing thin on me.

He suggested an incisional biopsy performed under general anesthetic. A larger tissue sample would be cut out and sent to a diagnostic laboratory in Texas that was rated as one of the best in the US.

The next day, Steve joined me in San José, and soon I was lying on a bed in the operation theatre's prep room, dressed in a surgical gown and hair net, watching as a nurse injected me with a "happy drug" to reduce anxiety while awaiting the procedure.

Dr. Heraldo appeared, all smiles. "Tranquila, Lokita, relajarse. It's going to be all fine. It's going to be all fine. Pura vida!"

"Pura Vida," or "pure life," is a motto in Costa Rica. It expresses a positive outlook on life, tranquility, and contentment, representing an appreciation for a simple and natural way of living, enjoying the beauty of nature, and finding joy in life's little pleasures.

Meanwhile, Steve was outside, and I could see his face through a porthole-style window. His eyes were wide with worry, and he bit his lips nervously. I tried to smile at him, waving and sending him love and kisses. There was nothing more we could offer each other. We were both weighed down by anxiety and fear, and I was about to go under the knife.

When I returned to consciousness, Dr. Heraldo told me he had removed a substantial amount of breast tissue and was sending it off to the lab in Texas that day.

Since the lump had been removed, there was no more pain in my breast, and I stayed in San José at a friend's house to rest, heal, and await the results. Steve returned to Montezuma to take care of our home and our dog.

My follow-up appointment was a week later.

"Buenos días, Lokita. Sí, come in," Dr. Heraldo said, inviting me into his office. "How are you?"

"Thanks, I'm okay. I've been taking it very easy, and now I'm ready to get back home to the beach, to Steve and Coco," I said.

He asked me to undress and then removed the bandage across my chest. Now I could see that much of the lower part of my left breast had been cut away, and there was a long, unsightly scar.

Dr. Heraldo nodded his approval. "Ah, que bueno, everything is healing well, muy bien," he assured me. We stood looking in the mirror together, and he added, "Later on, once you recover, we can do a nice reconstruction on your breast."

Then he asked me to sit down and, in the same conversational tone, announced, "I have some bad news."

I swallowed hard and, from far away, heard myself say, "Okay, what is it?"

"The samples were analyzed in the lab in Texas, and you have triple negative metaplastic carcinoma. This is a very rare type of breast cancer that grows and spreads rapidly."

I was stunned.

"This cancer doesn't respond to hormone therapy and is resistant to chemotherapy. The prognosis is bad, and you have only a slim chance of survival."

Shock. Fear. Disbelief.

He also told me that before and during the surgery, he had not considered the growth cancerous. Therefore, he didn't cut out the entire lump and didn't get "clear margins." It meant that the cancer was still in my breast.

This type of cancer wasn't the result of any gene my mother potentially passed down to me. It was an entirely different type and, as Dr. Heraldo pointed out, extremely rare.

"I'm terribly sorry," he added, "I want to apologize for not discovering it earlier."

Right. I had been his patient for seven months. And now he's sorry?

At that moment, I felt more indignant than terrified. "Let me get this straight. I've been leading a good life, eating the right food, doing enough exercise, happy with my husband, with a good sex life, a fulfilling career, and you're telling me I have deadly, untreatable cancer? Why did I get this?"

He just sat there, smiling patronizingly, almost kindly, as one would smile at a naughty little child, and in a casual manner said, "Oh, it's just bad luck."

Just bad luck?

In my lap, my hands curled into fists. Heat rose at the back of my neck and into my shoulders. I was ready to jump across the table, grab him by the scruff of the neck, and wipe that self-satisfied smile off his face.

First, he announced that everything was healing well and suggested a nice breast reconstruction. Then he handed me a death sentence and shrugged it off as bad luck.

With the wisdom of hindsight, I can see that, in a way, he was right. After making an in-depth study of my condition, I came to understand that there is no rhyme or reason for metaplastic triple negative carcinoma. It's not the consequence of bad diet, genetic predisposition, drug abuse, stress, lack of love, or even something as mystical as a closed heart chakra, which was once suggested to me.

Of course, it was tempting for me to speculate. Perhaps the stress of selling our home and letting go of our business could have triggered the cancer. Maybe the invasive nature of the biopsy had activated a malignancy that would have otherwise remained dormant, locked inside the scar tissue from the boil. But such speculation leads nowhere. The mind wants to find a reason, any reason, but the truth is that sometimes we simply do not know. And after a while I resolved not to burden myself with unnecessary self-blame and remorse.

Trying to gather my composure, I staggered out of the hospital into the hot, humid weather. I was petrified and bewildered. Nine long months of hell with biopsies, pain, ultrasound exams, different diagnoses, blood tests, creams, emotional stress, reassurances, etcetera—and now this.

Until then, I had thought I would act like my mother and not tell anybody should I ever receive a cancer diagnosis. But now all I wanted to do was call Steve.

"How was your visit with the doctor?"

"Steve, I have breast cancer."

We talked, but I don't remember what we said to each other. Shocked, I just stood there with the phone in my hand, unable to fully grasp what had just occurred. For nine months, nine long months, all the biopsy reports had been wrong.

Steve came to San José as quickly as he could, and we held each other close all night, crying softly together as our magnificent Costa Rican dream shattered into pieces.

We had intended this to be our ideal getaway retreat—making love, hanging out, working less, enjoying our dog, and being together in paradise. All our hopes had been crushed, and now, my health was gone.

"I have cancer…rare and untreatable cancer…I'm going to die…." The thoughts kept repeating in my mind like on a carousel, going round and round and round. Despite my best intentions, I did get lost in speculation.

"What have I done wrong? Why did I get cancer? Is it my fault? Did Mutti give it to me?" I desperately wanted someone, something, my mother, even myself, to be responsible, and yet there was simply no answer to these questions.

My nice, happy life was dissolving around me like an ice sculpture in the noonday sun. A veil of illusion had been ripped away, and new realizations were hurling themselves at me. I wasn't invincible. I could no longer presume I had plenty of time, that I would live until I was very old. Life is impermanent. Death is just around the corner. It had been much easier to live without thinking about death, without being reminded every moment that it's the direction in which we are all traveling. Now I was staring death in the face.

Given the grim prognosis, we wanted to be certain of what we were dealing with and decided to get a second opinion in the US. We had heard that there was excellent cancer care available in Marin County, California, an affluent area located north of San Francisco's Golden Gate Bridge, renowned for its sprawling headlands, old redwood trees, and glorious beaches.

Our first call was to our friend Paul, who was on the board of a local hospital that had a well-known cancer center. Steve and I had met Paul and his wife, Mary Alice, at Harbin in 2003, when they took several of our workshops. Over the years, a deep friendship had grown between us.

Fortunately, Paul was able to arrange an appointment at the cancer center on short notice.

This became our next move in the drama: return to the US, and if it was confirmed that I had metaplastic carcinoma, decide then on the next steps for treatment.

We no longer had a base in California. With our move to Costa Rica, we had given up everything—house, car, business—thinking that chapter of our lives was closed. Moreover, I had no health insurance, which would have been a huge obstacle without President Barack Obama's recently enacted "affordable care" program. Fortunately, people like me with pre-existing health conditions were now eligible for coverage.

My flight was booked, and I would be traveling alone since Steve needed to put the house in order and make arrangements for our potentially long-term absence.

While I was getting ready for my departure, we found ourselves with a week on our hands. Unexpectedly, this proved to be a wonderful time for us. There was no more stress, no more uncertainty, because now we knew the true identity of the creature in my breast.

Ignorance and confusion had been more difficult to deal with than the certainty that I had cancer. The diagnosis forced my mind to take a break from constant worry and speculation, and the hamster wheel of fear stood still, at least for a while.

Those days before I flew to California were a relief. We enjoyed our time. We rode our motorcycles, we went swimming, we played with the dog, we made love. The knowledge that everything was about to change heightened our appreciation of this honeymoon period, and we shared those few precious days just hanging out with each other.

I often thought of my mother then, riding the bicycle on that family excursion, and her light-hearted laughter and ecstasy as she sped across the busy intersection. I, too, could find joy amid these turbulent and frightening times, and it was one of the keys to life that Tantra taught me.

The darkness of the previous months had lifted, allowing us a week of freedom from worry. When we were given this special time to finally stop running around the medical circuit, to relax and stay home, we discovered once more the strength and delight of being in love. I look back on that week with such gratitude. They were the last carefree times that Steve and I would have together.

CHAPTER 5

ACCEPTING THE UNACCEPTABLE

From the beginning, I surrendered. I didn't fight the disease. Instead, I chose to embrace and accept it, which was different from the usual way of describing a person's relationship with cancer.

Obituaries often read, "He died after a long, hard battle with cancer." Or, if the patient survived, one might say, "She bravely fought the disease and won."

That wasn't me. Win or lose, I couldn't look at the disease that way. Being ill wasn't a war. It was important for me to accept the reality of the body. It lives and breathes according to the laws of nature. It strives to maintain a state of health but is vulnerable to disease and sickness, and one day it must die.

This doesn't mean I gave up. Not at all. I was determined to do everything I could to heal myself, but I refused to regard cancer as an enemy to be defeated. My new situation was, rather, a challenge to be understood, accepted, and transformed.

Tantra, as a spiritual practice, is defined as a tool for expansion—how can we grow and learn from the situations that life presents to us? It's thought that this lifetime is our opportunity to reach higher states of consciousness, spiritual enlightenment, and a state of equanimity in the face of our inevitable mortality. In this way, the Tantric perspective underpinned my approach to cancer.

On a practical level, finding a place to stay was easy. As soon as she heard I was coming to Marin, my best friend Bebe insisted I stay with her and her husband, Benny, in their home in San Rafael.

I had known Bebe for as long as I had known Steve. In fact, I had met her the same way: in an aquatic bodywork class in the pool at Harbin Hot Springs. Her long hair flowed in the water like a mermaid, her grace fascinated me, and her open, welcoming manner meant that the two of us soon started chatting and getting to know each other. Bebe embodied a blessing that she had received from her spiritual teacher, who told her, "Love is sweeter than honey." For the two of us, it certainly was.

Originally German and the same age as me, Bebe and Benny had been living in the US for some 28 years. Both were professional actors and magicians who entertained audiences of all ages with their clowning, mime, and puppetry. Bebe shared my passion for Watsu, and that day, during our first meeting in the pool, something clicked between us, which grew into a deep, long-lasting friendship.

A memory of a shopping trip with Bebe for work outfits still makes me smile. I was looking for sexy underwear and a long, dark red, silk robe for presenting a Tantric practice in a workshop while she was examining banana-shaped suits for Benny and herself for their walk-around street performances.

I loved visiting Bebe and Benny. Each time I came, he was practicing some new magic trick, keen to present it to me, a willing and captive audience. Once, during a public performance, he even cut me in half while I was inside a box!

"Herzlich willkommen in unserem Zuhause…welcome to our humble abode!" said Benny as Bebe and I arrived from the airport.

He, too, was German, and I felt right at home being able to speak my mother tongue with them.

They welcomed me with open hearts and open arms. Here, with them, I could gather the courage for the medical journey that lay ahead.

The prospect of receiving a second opinion at the cancer care center in Marin had raised my hopes. Maybe it was all a big mistake, a wrong diagnosis. Maybe it wasn't cancer after all, or maybe, at least, it was a better type than the one I had—if there can be such a thing as "a better cancer."

But first, I needed a car. In Marin, as in most parts of California, it's difficult to function without a car, and renting one didn't make financial sense. Buying a car was a stretch for me, though, as I knew practically nothing about them, and I was daunted by having to be responsible for this big-budget purchase without Steve. However, since I had no idea when he would be able to join me, I decided it was best to dive right in. I paid a visit to the car dealers at the auto mall an hour's drive up north and struck up a conversation with a friendly salesman named George.

Within minutes, I was telling him about living in Costa Rica, the Tantra teaching with Steve, and the cancer diagnosis. It's odd how sometimes we meet a stranger and instantly become friendly, telling intimate details of our lives while hardly knowing each other.

He showed me a secondhand, silver-colored VW Jetta station wagon in my price range, which he assured me was a solid and dependable vehicle. It had air conditioning, ample space at the back to let our *doghter* Coco sprawl out her long legs, and was one of those cars that could get dirty and still look okay. To me, it seemed perfect. I drove it, I liked it, I bought it. I was mobile.

Then my tests began at the cancer care center: PET/CT scans, MRIs, blood analysis, gene test, an EKG, another needle biopsy, and more. In addition, all my previous biopsy samples were reanalyzed, and some were sent to Stanford University Hospital for a third opinion.

Waiting for the medical results this time was the scariest experience so far because some of these tests would reveal whether the cancer had metastasized. It felt like a big storm was about to break loose. Every moment became precious. Every morsel of food I ate, every conversation I had, acquired new significance because the results would determine the quality of the rest of my life—and how long it might last.

However, there was to be no reprieve, no miracle, no proof of medical error. The diagnosis from the Texas lab I had received in Costa Rica was confirmed: triple negative metaplastic carcinoma, chemotherapy-resistant and very aggressive. The good news was that the cancer had not spread to other parts of my body.

There is something very final about a cancer diagnosis, especially if several pathologists have confirmed it. These were the cards I had been dealt, and all I could do now was try to play them right. There was no wiggle room, no escape. The body was ill, and in order to survive, something had to be done.

Bebe took me to my first appointment with the oncologist, Dr. Susanna Myers. She was in her mid-forties, friendly, with a gentle sense of humor, while at the same time serious about the disease and respectful of my concerns. She inspired trust and confidence that I could place my life in her hands.

"Frankly, in my entire career, I have only encountered four cases of this type of cancer," Dr. Susanna told me. "Two of those patients died; two of them are still alive."

"So, I guess it's a 50/50 split between life and death, then?"

When she nodded, I said half-jokingly, "I sure hope I'll be the one to tip the balance in favor of life!"

The prognosis was grim. I was given a 35 percent chance of surviving for two years after treatment.

She told me the medical plan: two cycles of chemotherapy, a unilateral mastectomy, and radiation. The chemotherapy would begin with four biweekly infusions of something called the "Red Devil" and be completed with twelve weekly infusions of a different drug cocktail.

In those first few weeks after the diagnosis, I received an avalanche of emails and messages from well-wishing friends and acquaintances urging me not to proceed with the conventional treatment but to explore alternative healing methods. Through our workshops, Steve and I had created an extensive network of contacts, and I regularly wrote a blog about my situation. In addition to good wishes and GoFundMe support, I got an abundance of advice.

People said to me, "Lokita, you're such a clean-living person. You shouldn't put this poison into your body…chemotherapy will kill you…I have a lot of experience with cancer patients as a homeopath… naturopath… spirit guide… listen, you can get a course of coffee enemas at this address…daily ozone injections will definitely kill the cancer…there's a long-distance healer called so-and-so in Brazil…eat only pineapples for the next three months, and the enzymes will destroy the cancerous cells…."

They had good intentions, but the implicit assumption that they knew best was hard for me to take. I may not have said it to anyone, but I was thinking, "Oh, yes, sure, and how do you know what's best for me? I'll take the traditional route for two reasons. One, because this is a very rare cancer that's notoriously hard to treat. And two, because most people I knew who used alternative therapies to treat cancer are now dead."

In many ways, my cancer journey was about learning to be my own best advocate under any circumstances and setting boundaries, not just with well-meaning advice-givers, but also with my husband.

For example, Steve would have preferred I undergo the treatment in Costa Rica. But I couldn't imagine traveling five hours to get a chemotherapy infusion, lying for six hours in a reclining chemo chair, traveling back for another five hours, and then sitting at home in the hot tropical climate far away from any doctor, not knowing what side effects would reveal themselves.

That was not going to work for me, so Steve suggested we could do the treatment in Mexico while staying with our friend Dennis, who had recently moved from California to a gorgeous beach house.

In many ways, this idea made sense. We had been friends with Dennis and Tracy for quite a few years, and they often visited us with their beloved Schnoodle Berkley. Having been successful in the marketing world, Dennis was a creative genius with a bottomless well of ideas that would bubble up abundantly whenever he became passionate about something, whether it was web design, video production, or photography. Dennis had helped us with our first, second, and third websites and was always available to nudge me in the right direction with marketing.

Tracy, a successful non-profit executive at an educational organization and a Pilates instructor, radiated calm and peacefulness, emphasized by her deep, warm voice and throaty laugh. An accomplished horsewoman and yoga practitioner, she was fit and toned and loved to be in nature. We went for many walks in the hills around our home, and on one of those walks, Tracy told me about their fantasy: They wanted us to marry them.

Steve and I liked the idea so much that we became ministers who could legally officiate weddings. The ceremony took place in a lovely Japanese garden in the South Bay area of San Francisco. As part of the ritual, we invited everyone to enter sacred time and sacred space with us to celebrate and bless this union. There were flowers everywhere and bees buzzing around, while the two lovers made their commitment to each other, surrounded by their loved ones. That special moment shall be etched forever into my memory.

Steve called them, and Dennis and Tracy were willing and welcoming.

"You can have the whole top floor of our house, and you can bring Coco, as well," they told us.

Steve really wanted that. "My love, it will be perfect for both of us. You can rest, enjoy the fresh air and watch the waves after your chemo, and I can go surfing and walk with Coco on the beach and take care of you."

I took a deep breath and pulled my shoulders back. "No, Steve, no. I need to be where I speak the language fluently, not my pidgin Spanish, not in a life and death situation."

This was one of the few times in all our years together that I had to stand my ground, put my foot down, and say, "No, Steve, this is not what's going to happen." Generally, his ideas were great, and I was willing to try them. Not this time.

I had to say the same thing to all my advice-givers. "Thank you, friends, but no. I alone decide what is best for me. This is my body; this is my life."

As much as I loved the closeness with others and relied on their support, I was reminded that I alone was responsible for my life and my body, making decisions and bearing the consequences.

It was strengthening to be my best advocate, but it was also hard. I was sick, I didn't know whether I would survive, and I was forced to stand up for myself in an extreme circumstance. Perhaps the most challenging thing of all was that I couldn't be certain I was doing the right thing. I was flying blind, trusting my gut, listening to my heart, and just hoping I was on the right track.

Before starting chemotherapy, I was asked to attend a meeting with my medical team, colloquially known as "chemo prep." Fortunately, Bebe came with me, radiating support the entire time, because this was the moment when the reality finally hit me. The next many months were going to be absolute hell.

We sat around the table in a nondescript conference room, a couple of doctors and chemo nurses, Bebe, and me. The room was lit with bright fluorescent lights. My notepad was open in front of me, the pen poised in my hand.

After the brief welcome and introductions, the information began hailing down on me. "You'll feel nauseous and throw up a lot. You'll lose your hair, have no energy, and be unable to eat. Your mouth is going to swell up, your head is going to hurt, you are going to lose weight. Your nails might blacken and fall out." On and on it went, one thing after another.

Their words bombarded me, and there was no escape. "You'll receive steroids and medications against nausea, constipation, and fatigue. For sleeping, we'll give you anti-anxiety medication."

In addition to the chemo sessions, there would be appointments for blood tests, platelet infusions, booster injections, cell counts, and other unforeseeable issues. One thing I knew: This intense process would never have worked in Costa Rica or Mexico. I could barely comprehend it all in English.

The medical team had given this chemo prep talk many times, and I didn't envy them. The looks on their faces mirrored their concern and compassion.

"Should your white blood cells drop to a certain level, chemo infusions will have to be stopped until your blood improves."

That was the last thing I needed to hear. I wanted a firm schedule on which I could rely. Steps one, two, and three. Then it would be over, and Steve and I could return to Costa Rica.

When we walked into the meeting, I stood tall. When the talk was over, I felt roughed up. My strength was gone, and my head hung low. The Lokita I knew was no longer there in the hospital conference room, nor could she be found for the remainder of the day. Instead, there was a grey, sad person, a bundle of doubts and fears.

But the bottom line was unavoidable. I had to keep going if I wanted to survive. I was willing to try everything.

Twice, I participated in a support group facilitated by a psychotherapist for women with a breast cancer diagnosis. My expectation had been one of kinship and mutual understanding. I was looking forward to being with others going through the same things. However, it turned out quite differently.

In the circle of ten women, each talked for a few minutes about their feelings, their diagnosis, and their treatment plans. One woman had a tiny tumor removed in a simple procedure, but she was worried cancer would return. Another woman had a tumor removed and needed radiation. Yet another had to have a total of four chemotherapy infusions. They all lamented bitterly, were scared and worried.

But none of them had a cancer as terrible as mine. None of them had to go through such an extensive, long treatment plan as my oncologist had proposed. None of these women were as close to death as I was.

For the first time on this cancer journey, hot fury and anger boiled up inside me. How could they complain about their little cancers when I was plunging into such hellfire? Why couldn't they be happy and grateful that they had simple situations to deal with? This "support" group was a waste of my time.

Of course, I didn't say these things out loud, but I was fired up inside and left the group feeling angry, bitter, and self-righteous.

I needed to let off some steam. Fortunately, I could do that with my kind and understanding friends. Yet, those feelings of rage and intolerance were part of having cancer, and to cultivate inner stability, I had to accept them. Sometimes, I would feel clear and accepting, while at other times, I would be angry and frustrated. The best thing I could do for myself was to accept my emotions, let them wash over me, be thrown around by them, and then let them go. When I was angry, I was angry. When I was clear, I was that. At the same time, I was able to experience myself as a spectator rather than being consumed by and identifying with those emotions. It was a knack I'd learned over the years through practicing various meditation techniques—not going up and down like a yo-yo but abiding in the middle of these mood swings. Again and again, I found true equanimity and inner peace.

The second support group meeting I attended was quite different, probably because I had burned through the fury by then and could share the wisdom I had gained. One woman, while sharing, got into a very emotional state, crying and breaking down, and I felt like an elder who could help her through this nightmare of emotions and come out the other side. The meeting ended with hugs and love. Nevertheless, I never went back for another one.

My first chemo session was on August 20th, 2015. Steve had not yet arrived from Costa Rica, and I was still living with Bebe and Benny in San Rafael. Right before the infusion, Bebe and I met with Dr. Susanna.

"Today, and three more times, you will receive a bright orange chemical mix we call the Red Devil," she informed me. "It's so toxic that we can't put it into your veins directly because if it accidentally touches your skin, it will burn you. Instead, it gets injected into a drip line."

First came the anti-allergy medicine, then the steroids, and finally, the Red Devil. I lay on the chemotherapy recliner, watching the orange liquid slowly flow down the line and disappear into my body.

At that moment, I remembered my decision to accept the disease and surrender to the process. The word "surrender" has interesting origins. It means to give oneself over to a higher power, which to me signified a universal force greater than me or cancer. And so the Red Devil became a healing elixir created by the genius of medical science to cure me.

"May this golden elixir heal me," I repeated to myself. "I'm receiving this elixir to heal the cancer so I may live."

I knew I would soon be suffering from the side effects of the chemo drugs, but at least for that moment, I felt at peace.

"Okay," I said to myself. "From a place of gentleness and grace, with as much calm as I can muster, with all my heart, in all humility, I surrender to this process."

As a support, I listened to discourses by the mystic Osho, whom I had met personally some 30 years earlier. This was helpful, not because of any spiritual teaching his words could impart, but because, through listening to the quality of his voice, I could connect to a space beyond the words—the same universal space to which I was giving myself. It was another door to the same "beyond."

After the first treatment ended, I felt surprisingly well and in good spirits. A great weight had been lifted off my mind. Finally, I received a correct diagnosis—confirmed by several medical teams—and began treatment. Especially since the cancer was aggressive and fast-growing, time was of the essence, and action was a relief.

The tidal wave of side effects hit after I returned home and enthusiastically wolfed down a salad and some fruit for lunch. Bad idea! I turned into a complete zombie, sick to my stomach and so dizzy I couldn't even sit up. My spiritual ideas went straight out the window, and the "golden elixir" turned into a dark, nasty poison. I called Dr. Susanna, and she suggested I just sleep it off.

For the next 24 hours, I floated in a daze between dreamless sleep and being half awake, in which my body and my consciousness parted company, and I sensed that "I am not my body."

When I came back to consciousness, I dragged myself to the bathroom to vomit. My mouth felt like it was filled with fur.

The days following my first chemo treatment blurred into a thick fog. In contrast to feeling "I am not my body," the strongest experience now was that my body took over completely. I felt I was nothing but the body because it required every ounce of my energy to handle the chemicals with which it had been infused.

A message came from Steve that he was arriving on August 25th, five days after my first chemo session, so I had time to partially recover and prepare to move to a new place. It was clear we couldn't continue to live with Bebe and Benny. Steve was coming with Coco, and their house wasn't suitable for the five of us.

As chance would have it, our friend Mary Alice and her husband Paul, who had organized my first appointment with the specialist at the cancer care center, invited us to stay in their spacious home in San Geronimo, a rural enclave just outside of nearby Fairfax. Adjacent to the main house, they had a separate bungalow ideal for Steve, Coco, and me.

This was nothing short of a miracle. We had been fretting about where we would live and how much rent we would have to pay, and although my intuition told me that everything would work out, I had no idea how it might happen until Paul and Mary Alice approached me with their offer.

An attractive man in his early sixties, Paul could illuminate any room with his bright smile, charm, and ready wit. Having been successful in the corporate world, he retired in 2008 and, among various charitable activities, served as the chairman of a local hospital. He was dedicated to living his best life with his wife and family.

His wife, Mary Alice, was unflappable. She had a deep voice, silvery blonde hair, and a dry sense of humor that could have me in stitches in no time. Her heart was in the right place, and you could always rely on Mary Alice to tell the truth, whether you liked it or not. Steve and I were close to both of them, and they offered us a safe haven when we needed it the most.

Before Steve arrived, I faced another challenge. Should I cut my long, shiny blonde hair that would fall out as a side effect of the chemotherapy? For many years it had been part of my self-image as an attractive woman. I would feel especially gorgeous when I sashayed into the workshop room in a flowing dress with my long hair swishing around me like golden silk threads.

My hair had become part of my identity. Now it would have to go.

After receiving the cancer diagnosis, I joined a Facebook group of some twelve hundred women from around the world who, like me, had been diagnosed with this rare form of cancer and were in various stages of treatment or remission. This group provided me with a wealth of support and knowledge. For example, I learned that typically after the second Red Devil infusion, the hair would start to fall out.

Bebe took me to a hair salon and held my hand as I sat there with my eyes closed while the hairdresser cut it all off.

Finally, I opened my eyes and looked in the mirror. There I saw a new woman and felt like a new woman, too. My hair looked cute and attractive, light and feathery, and, of course, incredibly easy to manage. It also added to the ongoing "Great Dissolution," in which a whole lot of my usual "Lokita-ness" was being stripped away.

So, when I picked up Steve from the airport, I had short hair, which he had never seen before. I looked at least ten years younger, almost like a boy, because I was already quite slim, even before the chemo had taken away my appetite.

On the day of our reunion, I schlepped myself to the airport in San Francisco, allowing three hours for the 75-minute drive, with lots of extra time to pull off the freeway and rest. There was just no way I was *not* going to pick up Steve and Coco.

We had been apart for three weeks, and when they walked out of the elevator, my heart lurched, and everything suddenly felt better. Even though I was in a chemo-induced fog and feeling weak, my heart beat vigorously, overflowing with the love and joy of being with my family again.

Tears rolled down my cheeks. "Oh, my love, it's so good to see you again!" I murmured, hugging him as tightly as I could.

"Let me take a look at your new hair." I turned 360 degrees to show off for him. "Wow, it looks amazing! You're beautiful with short hair, and I love you exactly the way you are."

He complimented me on looking so radiant and vibrant. I was over the moon to be with him again.

Steve put his bags in the back of the Jetta, showed Coco her place, and slid into the driver's seat while I took the passenger seat. We cruised out onto the freeway.

For me, things couldn't have been better, given the circumstances. It was a lovely day, and in the distance, the skyscrapers of downtown San Francisco reflected the golden rays of the setting sun. The air smelled like eucalyptus trees and bay leaves. I leaned back and relaxed. Steve was finally here.

But for Steve, a problem soon developed: the car. It didn't live up to his standards, and even though he was delighted to see me, his "inner mechanic" couldn't resist registering a complaint.

"What's the matter with this thing?" he grunted, shifting gears and slapping the steering wheel. "The shocks are worn out, and the brakes need adjusting...."

"I did the best I could," I protested. "What do you expect for four thousand bucks? It's a good, practical car."

"Okay, sorry, my love, it was a long flight, and I'm exhausted. I didn't mean to upset you. We'll get it checked out later."

Soon afterwards, we had to replace the shock absorbers and brakes and buy new tires, but Steve had to admit the Jetta was perfect for our purpose. He was particularly pleased about the roof rack—ideal for his surfboard.

Over the next few days, we made ourselves at home in the bungalow at Paul and Mary Alice's house and settled into a sweet routine.

Steve would practice yoga, swim in the pool, go for walks with Coco, provide entertainment and take care of me whenever I needed anything. I would occasionally shop for food, but mainly I would just hang out because I had little or no energy, although I did manage a little gardening once in a while. Together we would enjoy balmy evenings, sometimes with Paul and Mary Alice, sometimes with other friends who visited.

On Mondays, if I felt strong enough, we would visit the nearby Spirit Rock Meditation Center, a Buddhist institute, where a talk on the Dharma teachings of Gautam Buddha was offered to the public, followed by 45 minutes of meditation.

One night, the presenter spoke about "post-traumatic growth," a concept that was becoming popular in New Age circles and that I was familiar with. Yet try as I might, here and now, I couldn't see beyond the trauma to the growth part. How could I look ahead to future growth when all my resources were needed just to survive the present? I had to deal with very down-to-earth, practical, immediate matters like, for example, losing my precious golden locks, as Steve liked to call my hair.

By now, it was beginning to fall out in tufts. I went to the hairdresser again with Bebe, and this time it all had to go. No more boyish looks, just a bald-headed Lokita staring back at me in the mirror after the full shave.

Afterwards, Bebe took me to a costume shop and helped me choose a wig that matched my natural hair color and style. Then we went back to her house, and she dug out a box filled with wigs from her performances, allowing me to try every style imaginable: long white curly locks, fluffy pink hair, smooth dark tresses....

It was a fun moment, but I also felt okay being bald. It was my statement to the world: "I'm going through cancer treatment, and as long as I can walk around without a hat because the weather is warm enough, I'm not going to hide what's going on with me."

People would look at me in the street, and I could read the thoughts in their eyes. "Oh dear, poor woman. She has cancer. And so young!" I could see the movie going on inside their heads and the fear that accompanied it—maybe one day, it might happen to them, too.

It was not my intention to confront people by exposing my head. Quite simply, the wig felt scratchy on my scalp, and I preferred not to wear it.

Hair loss is one of the most common side effects of chemotherapy. I had only ever thought about it in terms of the hair on my head, and it had never occurred to me that losing hair meant losing every single hair on my body! For example, my pubic and armpit hair disappeared, and my eyebrows and eyelashes fell out, giving me a new look. I could have anticipated all this had I thought it through, but losing the tiny hairs inside my nostrils came as a real surprise. I realized it only when my nose became constantly runny, which was awkward, to say the least.

Also, the soft, fuzzy hair on my face vanished, and I didn't even notice its absence until it regrew months after chemo, when an esthetician humorously called me her "wolverine." Indeed, for a few weeks, I felt like a werewolf, with long, fuzzy blonde hair growing on my cheeks. The esthetician wanted to wax it off, but I was so happy with the reappearance of any kind of hair that I didn't allow her to.

As for Steve, he repeatedly assured me that my eyes shone brightly and that I was beautiful whether I had hair or not. But he added, "You must get a tan on your naked head!"

Unfortunately, this wasn't an option because when undergoing chemotherapy, exposure to sun is not recommended.

On several occasions, Steve and I drove to Bolinas, a picturesque little town on the Pacific coast, a thirty-minute drive from where we lived. Steve loved surfing, and I would sit in a small tent at the back of the beach to keep out of the wind and sun, watching him riding the waves and waiting with Coco for him to come back to us.

I would eat watermelon slices, one of the few foods I could tolerate, and happily stay there, absorbing the regenerating power of the ocean air flowing into my body.

Three weeks after Steve arrived, we received a shock. The evening news reported that a huge wildfire had broken out in Northern California and was sweeping through Lake County. Driven by strong winds, Harbin Hot Springs lay directly in its path.

As we watched the news of the devastating wall of flames, Steve still held out hope, assuring me, "No, no, they'll save some of the buildings."

But the fire, known as the "Valley Fire," was unstoppable and became the third largest in California's history. Once it reached the canyon where Harbin was located, it burned all the buildings and the vegetation to the ground, destroying much of Middletown, the small nearby town. The home we had sold a few months earlier miraculously survived untouched.

We spent the evening frantically contacting friends who had been living in the area, making sure they had gotten out okay. One friend said the fire roared into the canyon so fast she barely had time to grab her cat and her computer, jump in the car, and escape. Everything else went up in smoke.

Harbin had been an integral part of our lives and especially our teaching for so many years. Thousands of people were touched and transformed by our seminars, and by the work of so many other spiritual teachers, in this sacred place, in the healing waters, in the cozy seminar buildings.

We had enjoyed years and years of incredible experiences there, and now... poof! One large, furious fire ate it all up. To me, it was yet another step in the dissolution of everything I held dear. First our house, then our business, then my health, and now Harbin. What else could be taken away from me? Enough already!

The fourth and last infusion of the Red Devil was administered on October 1st, and afterward, I was more tired than ever before. For days, I could hardly get out of bed. I couldn't eat anything; I was just so sick.

One afternoon, I sat in the garden utterly exhausted while Steve and Paul puttered around, discussing what to plant. As I noticed the cool breeze on my skin and listened to the birds singing, I thought, "Well, Lokita, we're all still alive until we die." Until the very last breath, there's still life flowing in our veins. If all I could do was sit there, taking in the sensations of life around me, that would be plenty for now.

Then came the evening of Sunday, October 4th. After dinner, we were sitting happily together, Steve, Paul and Mary Alice, Coco, and me. I had started knitting again and was creating a scarf for Steve.

We talked about Harbin and the great times we had experienced there. We told the stories of how we met, talked about funny moments in our marriages, and enjoyed reminiscing and sharing stories like old friends do. It was cozy, heartwarming, and fun. Paul, Mary Alice, and I still sometimes talk about the special nature of that evening, when somehow, without any conscious intent, we felt so in tune with each other, so harmonious.

It was getting late. I was tired from the chemo, and we had laughed a lot, which was a lovely but exhausting experience.

Steve and I went to our bedroom. There was no lovemaking on our agenda. I had no hair, no energy, and was nothing but skin and bone, weighing barely 95 pounds.

No, we were just going to lie on the bed, relax, and slowly fall asleep. Steve was lying on his back, and I was lying inside his arm, his "wing," as I liked to call it, where I could snuggle up against him. He had this special place in his shoulder that my head, the side of my chin, and my cheek could nestle in.

At one point, I pushed myself up on my elbow and looked at Steve's beloved face with those vulnerable blue eyes, reminding me how fortunate I was to be with this caring, loving man.

There was something on my mind that I needed to share.

"Steve, you do realize that I'm really, really ill?"

In the past, during our intimate bedtime talks, Steve had often mentioned that he, being 15 years my senior, would most likely die before me. In the natural order of things, that's how one would expect things to go.

But cancer had reversed our roles, and I found myself saying to him, "Let's face it. I might not be here much longer. I may not be able to go back to Costa Rica with you. Maybe I won't make it, Steve, seriously. Maybe I'll die."

Steve wanted to reassure me. "Oh, my love, please don't talk like that. That is definitely not going to happen. You're coming back with me when your treatment finishes in April."

I felt calm about it but also insistent. "I want you to know how much I love you, and I'm so sorry…."

I'll never forget that moment. Even to this day, it still chokes me up. I apologized and said, "Steve, I'm so sorry I ruined the Costa Rican dream for you. I know how much you wanted it, and I'm sorry that my illness came in the way.

"If you want to go back to Costa Rica, I can totally understand it. In fact, I almost want you to go back because you wished for it so much and for so long. You don't need to see me here like this. I can do this on my own, and I'll come to Costa Rica when I'm done in April."

Yes, Steve wanted to be with me because he loved me and was committed to standing by me in good times and bad times. But he was unhappy in Marin. He really didn't want to be there.

Steve flat-out refused. "No, I'll stay here with you. Whatever happens, we'll pull through this. We're one thing, remember? Let's hold the vision that we'll go back to Costa Rica together when this is over."

We talked a bit more. I remember saying how grateful I was to him for the love we shared. We were that kind of couple. Over the years, we had always taken the time to value and appreciate each other.

Before one of us went somewhere without the other, even if it were only for a short trip to the grocery store, we would make sure to say a proper goodbye. We wouldn't just shut the door and leave.

Nobody can predict when we'll share our last kiss with our partner, give a final embrace to our best friend, or see our family for the last time. What we can all be sure of is that one day, it really will be the last time, and it's not given to us to know when that will be.

Steve and I kissed each other goodnight several times. In between, we talked a bit more about how this cancer experience was scary for both of us, but we trusted we could pull through it together.

The last thing I said was, "Even if I have to die and leave this body, then so be it. In some way, it will be fine, too." Not that I considered it a great prospect, but in the spirit of acceptance, I was saying, "Ah well, if this is what the universe has in mind for me, so it shall be."

We held each other close and fell asleep in a tender, loving, and sweet way. That was the night of October 4th, 2015.

CHAPTER 6

THREE TOTAL STRANGERS

October 5th was a lovely Indian summer day in Northern California, and I was sitting outside in the garden, lounging in a comfy, padded chair. I had nothing to do, simply because I wasn't capable of doing anything, so exhausted was I from the chemotherapy.

In the early afternoon, Steve sat down with me, buzzing with energy. "My love, I've got an idea. Let's take Coco to Bolinas beach. I'll bring my surfboard and ride some waves, and you can enjoy the sunshine and ocean air. It'll do you good."

I shook my head. "Sorry, Steve. I can't go. I'm completely exhausted. If you want to go, it'll have to be a solo trip this time."

"Well, okay then, I won't go. I'll find something else to do."

Since then, I have wondered many times if he would have averted his tragic fate had he decided to make the trip to Bolinas without me or if I had agreed to join him, but we'll never know the answer to that unanswerable question.

The frown on his forehead and his tightlipped smile told me he was annoyed that I didn't want to come. I knew Steve was finding it difficult to be in this supportive role. He was doing his best, and for me couldn't have been a better husband under these scary and uncertain circumstances. Yet it was hard for him.

Steve's philosophy was that people couldn't help others unless they cared for themselves first. In general, I understood and appreciated this concept. Yet now that I was most vulnerable and needed support, it appeared selfish.

Before I got sick, if he suggested something that I might not have wanted to do, more often than not, I would join him anyway. But now, I had no choice but to recognize and communicate my boundaries. Steve was meeting a new Lokita, and this wasn't easy for him.

He gave up on Bolinas and focused on creating a new irrigation system for the garden, discussing the project with Paul and making a list of items he needed to buy while Coco gently nuzzled his leg. I lazily took a couple of photos of the three of them. They looked gorgeous standing together in the garden, bathed in golden light—two handsome men and a dog.

A little later, Steve came over to me and hugged me. "Okay, my love, I'm off to Fairfax to get cash from the ATM, and then I'll take the dog for a walk. Paul told me about a trail that I'm going to explore with Coco. I'll be back soon, and we'll go to Spirit Rock at seven."

"Sounds great! Have fun!"

He kissed me goodbye, got in the car with Coco, and drove off.

That was around 3:30 in the afternoon. Eventually, the sun started sinking, and I joined Mary Alice in the kitchen, where she was preparing dinner.

Just before six o'clock, Steve texted me: "Hi, sweetie. I'll be home soon. We'll have a bite to eat, then I'll take you to Spirit Rock."

I texted back: "Okay. Not sure I can go. Still exhausted. Anyway, come home. We'll figure it out."

But Steve didn't come home.

Paul, Mary Alice, and I ate our dinner.

"Hmm, what happened to Steve?" Paul wondered aloud as he collected the plates. "It's past seven already."

I folded my napkin. "Yes, strange that he's not here yet. I'll give him a call." Steve didn't pick up. "I guess his ringer is turned off."

We finished clearing the dining table. Mary Alice knew Steve would have alerted me if he wasn't coming home for dinner.

"This is very weird. Maybe he's gone to Spirit Rock by himself," she said.

"Yes, after reading my text, maybe he thought I wasn't coming, so he ate something in Fairfax and went alone. Anyway, he'll probably be home soon."

I hugged Paul and Mary Alice. "I'm off to bed. See you in the morning."

Over the next couple of hours, I called Steve several more times. But there was no answer. I was bone-tired and fell asleep. Then, just before 3:00 am, I woke up. Steve was not in bed beside me.

"Perhaps he's in the bathroom?" I wondered, then noticed, "Oh, but the dog's not here, either. Where's Coco?" Then I looked out the window across the carport. It was empty.

Now I began to get scared. Steve would never stay away this long without telling me.

I went online, checking the California Highway Patrol's website.

"Perhaps he was involved in a car crash and taken to hospital?" I said aloud into the dark.

But no, there was no mention of any accident.

I started pacing around the room in my bathrobe.

"Where is he? What could have happened to him? What can I do?" My head was spinning. "Should I call Bebe? She might know what to do." But it was 3:30 am, and she was sleeping. Instead, I phoned my sister Wiebke in Denmark, where it was already close to midday. I had to talk to someone.

"Steve hasn't come home all night, and I don't know where he is." My voice was trembling, my mouth suddenly dry. "He took Coco for a walk in the afternoon. The car isn't here. There are no accident reports. What should I do?" I could hear my despair echoing back to me through the line.

Then there was a knock on my door, and Mary Alice stood there, stone-faced.

"Lokita, you better come downstairs."

I quickly told my sister, "I have to go. Mary Alice is at the bedroom door. Something strange is happening."

I hung up, went into the main house, and was confronted with a scene straight out of a movie. Four police officers in full uniform were standing in the hallway. For a seemingly endless moment, they all looked at me.

"Are you Mrs. Carter?"

"Yes, I'm Lokita Carter." A sudden chill washed over me.

"Well, Mrs. Carter, please come and sit down."

At that moment, the worst scenario that ran through my mind was that Steve must be in the ICU at some hospital.

We sat down at the dining table. Paul and Mary Alice were there in their bathrobes, their faces ashen.

"Mrs. Carter, we have some very unfortunate news."

I froze. The silence was deafening.

"Your husband was found shot dead on Gunshot Fire Road in Fairfax. Your dog was also shot but is expected to recover."

Gunshot Fire Road? Steve dead? Coco shot? I stared at them.

"You have got to be kidding me!" I stood up, hands on my hips, taking on an almost aggressive stance, angry and scared at the same time. Rubbing my bald head, I shouted, "Look, I have no hair! I have cancer! If this is an episode of Hidden Camera, it's not funny! Why are you doing this to me?"

The police officer, who identified himself as Scott, spoke in a soft, deep voice. "We're so very sorry, Mrs. Carter. This is not a Hidden Camera episode. Your husband is dead."

Time stood still. Paul and Mary Alice burst into tears. From far away, I heard myself ask, "What happened?"

"Well, we don't know very much yet. Your husband was found around 6:00 pm on the trail."

They told me what they knew, but some details came later, so I'm not sure how much of the following information I received in that first terrible hour. Here is what I learned:

At about six o'clock, shortly after Steve sent me the text message, a young hiker found Steve dead close to the entrance to the trail. He was lying bleeding on the ground, and Coco was standing next to him, crying and bleeding. The hiker immediately called 911.

When the police arrived, they discovered that both Steve and Coco had been shot. Whoever killed Steve had taken the car, his wallet, and his phone, so there was no immediate way to identify him, and that's why it took so long to inform me, the police officer explained.

Within minutes, there was a huge police presence on the trail: helicopters, cars with flashing blue lights, a fire truck, an ambulance with first responders, and so forth. Reports from local witnesses indicated that three scruffy-looking young people, two men and a woman, had been acting suspiciously in the area shortly before the murder.

I found out later how the police located me. Coco had a tag on her collar with our Costa Rican phone number and Steve's name. But they didn't know who he was or where he lived.

A Google search revealed Steve's name in the text of my online blog. There were also some photos of Coco, so the detectives realized they had found him, I was his wife, and we were Tantra teachers. The only contact detail was a website form: "To write now, click here."

In one of my blog posts, the detectives discovered a mention of a friend who was the chairman of the local hospital and lived in San Geronimo. They made calls to hospital personnel until they found Paul, and finally, through him, they were able to reach me.

The police officers left. Our eyes were glazed over, our bodies stiff from the impact of the shocking news. Steve was dead. He was shot dead. He was murdered.

Mary Alice was the first to move. "You have to make some calls, Lokita. I'll go get the phone."

Numbed and functioning purely on automatic, I called my sister and then Bebe, who within minutes arrived at the house with Benny and sat with us at the dining table. They had known Steve for almost 30 years. Now Steve was no longer with us. He had been murdered in cold blood.

I called Steve's first wife and begged her to tell their children, both adults. It would be better if they received the news from their mother, who lived in the same town and could be there with them. I also called one of Steve's brothers.

Finally, I called Scott, the police detective, to confirm that the closest family had been informed of the murder and that Steve's name could now be given to the media.

Up to this point, I had been paralyzed with shock, barely able to grasp what had happened but needing to make the necessary calls. There were no tears, no emotion. But then, suddenly, it all rose up in me at once. My body took over, and I ran into the laundry room and locked the door.

I went berserk, kicking the dryer, hitting the washing machine with my fists, crying and howling in anguish, yelling, "Steve is dead! My love is dead! What am I going to do? I want to be dead, too! Why not me? If I had only gone to Bolinas with him!"

My friends stood outside the door, and I could hear them shouting and rattling the door handle. "Lokita, can we help you? Open up! Are you okay in there?"

I was beside myself, broken open, screaming, "Leave me alone!"

All my anger, grief, and devastation went into that laundry room until, eventually, I was spent. I had nothing left. I weighed nothing. I was a skin-covered skeleton with no hair. In fact, I had nothing left to begin with. Yet I still had enough energy to vent my emotions in that laundry room.

With my last bit of strength, I finally opened the door and staggered upstairs to our bedroom. There, I fell on the floor, sobbing, "I don't want to live anymore. I want to die. I don't want to live." I repeated it over and over again, bawling my eyes out.

Never again could I touch Steve's warm skin. Never again smell his manly scent. Never again snuggle up in his wing. Never again hear his cheerful voice calling out for me, "My love, where are you?" Never again could we make love. Never again would he hold my hand. Never again would we be one thing. Never again could I eat his favorite brown rice with beans or taste his special anniversary fruit salad laced with a sip of Bailey's. Never again would he write "Happy birthday my love" on the table with tropical flowers when I woke up. Never again would he swish me around and around when dancing his version of Salsa.

Steve was gone, and Coco was shot. But apparently, she was still alive. "Where is Coco? Where's my dog? Where is she?" I can still hear the despair in my voice as I repeatedly asked that question. At that moment, Coco was my last thread of hope to go on living.

"We don't know, Lokita," Mary Alice had come into the bedroom. "But we will find out. I'll call a friend. She has some contacts that could help us."

Timo, Mary Alice's friend, came by later in the morning.

"My heartfelt condolences, Lokita. I can't even begin to imagine what you must be going through now. I'll do everything I can to find out where Coco is."

Even today, tears still come to my eyes when I remember how kind everyone was, so many people reaching out to me, willing to help in whatever way they could. It was a miracle of human love and kindness in light of a terrible tragedy.

Finding Coco was no easy task. This was a murder investigation, and the police regarded her as evidence of what had occurred on the trail that evening. Therefore, Coco had to be shielded from public view.

But Timo was persistent in her efforts, knocking on many official doors. In the end, she could confirm Coco's whereabouts, presumably by convincing the authorities that it was important for my fragile well-being.

Coco had been taken under the wing of the Marin Humane Society, whose Director of Animal Services, Cindy Machado, had made Coco's survival her top priority. Once she and her team learned the identity of the dog and the circumstances of the murder, they were thinking along lines similar to Timo. "The woman has cancer, and her husband was just murdered, so we have to save this dog, whatever the cost."

At first, Coco was transported to an emergency veterinary clinic in San Rafael, where they immediately operated on her. She had been shot directly in the right eye at close range, and the bullet had passed through her face, shattering her left lower jaw.

But there was another problem. Coco was diagnosed with Von Willebrand disease, a bleeding disorder typical for Dobermans, whereby the blood does not coagulate. She was given blood transfusions, but she didn't stop bleeding.

From San Rafael, she was taken to UC Davis, where there is a big veterinary teaching hospital. Coco was rushed into intensive care. After receiving several more blood transfusions, her condition stabilized, and she was pronounced out of immediate danger.

Meanwhile, the media was going crazy. When somebody gets murdered, there is inevitably press interest. But when somebody gets murdered in Marin County, one of the wealthiest areas in California, on a public trail where anyone could have been walking, that's front-page news.

It was all over the television news channels. "Steve Carter... Tantra instructor... shot dead... grieving widow with cancer... dog also shot but will survive... three suspects... car missing...."

Media attention continued for days, even spreading to other countries. Friends from Denmark phoned and said, "We just saw the news!" A friend from England called me saying, "Oh, Lokita, I am so sorry! I just watched BBC."

Public interest was immense, and so was the compassion and sensitivity of the journalists. Contrary to most mainstream media portrayals, the reports about Steve's murder never contained anything salacious about Tantra. There was nothing but respectfulness for "the Tantra Yoga instructor whose wife is cancer-stricken...."

In the afternoon of that first day, two police officers, Scott and Adam, came by again to interview me.

"Did Steve have any enemies? What kind of car did you have? At what time did you see him last? Why did he go to Fairfax, and what was he doing on the hiking trail?" They did their job as best they could, but for me, it was pure hell.

The next day, October 7th, I received a call from Scott, wanting to know where we had bought the car. A short while later, he called again.

"We need your permission for something," he began.

"For what?" I mumbled.

"We have been informed that the car has a GPS installed."

George, the car salesman, had seen the news, remembered me, and informed the police that the car I bought from him had been fitted with a commercial tracking system installed as a precaution against theft or loan default. At the time of purchase, George hadn't told me about it, probably thinking it wasn't important since I was paying cash up front.

"The tracking system was deactivated when you bought the car. Now, we must ask you, as the owner, for permission to turn the system back on and track the vehicle."

"Yes." I saw a glimmer of hope that those responsible for Steve's death could be caught. "Yes, of course."

So, the car I had bought and which Steve hadn't liked was the key to locating his killers.

Not long after that conversation, I was sitting in my room with Bebe when the phone rang once more.

It was Scott. "Lokita, the car was found. It was parked outside a public dining hall in Portland, Oregon. The three suspects were inside eating and have been arrested. Please don't speak about it to anyone yet. I'll be in touch again soon."

Inside the car, Scott told me, police officers found a tent, passport, and personal belongings of Audrey Carey, the 23-year-old Canadian backpacker who had been murdered in San Francisco's

Golden Gate Park three days before Steve's death. These killers had murdered not just once but twice.

Usually, I told Bebe everything. She knew me more intimately than anyone other than Steve. As I disconnected the call, I looked at my best friend, knowing that this time, I couldn't tell her what was going on. At least for the moment, I could only hope that she sensed my relief. She stood up, came over to me, and hugged me.

More details emerged as reports came in from the public. A gas station attendant at Point Reyes remembered three young people stopping to buy gas, cigarettes, and chips with wet $20 bills. One of the three had told him the bills were wet because his mother had accidentally washed the money with his clothes. Later, after watching the news, the attendant figured these were the suspects. The notes had been stained with Steve's blood and were quickly washed by the suspects in the gas station's bathroom.

In another report, a woman picking up her children from school in Fairfax noticed three "grungy" young people lurking around the campus that afternoon. She found them so suspicious that she took their picture, which appeared to match the three murder suspects.

Steve was dead. Shot.

These drifters obviously wanted a car and money, but why shoot their chosen victim? Why rob an innocent man of his life, and for what—a nondescript, second-hand, unremarkable car?

Steve was easygoing, laid back, and friendly. It didn't take much to imagine a more plausible scene. He's walking along with Coco, having a good time, it's a beautiful day, he's going back to his wife, dinner will be ready, until....

Some thieves jump out of the bushes with a gun and say, "Hey, old man, give us your car key!" What would Steve say? "Oh, you want my car key? Sure, here it is. No problem. You want my wallet too? Take it. Look, here's two hundred dollars. Good luck!" But that's not what happened.

As the story unfolded, hour after hour, with no let-up, the strain on me and my close friends became severe, and I realized I needed more emotional support to help me get through the days ahead. Instinctively, I called Roger, a good friend from Harbin who had lost everything in the Valley Fire and was staying temporarily in Grass Valley, California.

Roger was a warm-hearted man with a cheerful face, trim beard, and compassionate brown eyes. The fact that we shared a similar background in spirituality and meditation made our friendship easy and deep. We never had to explain much because we intuitively understood each other.

I called him, told him what had happened, and asked if he could come and be with me. He flung his few remaining belongings in the back of his car and was with us a few hours later. Paul and Mary Alice welcomed Roger warmly. They set up a bedroom for him, and he stayed with us for two weeks.

Although Roger had been a friend to Steve and me, he hadn't been particularly close to Steve. While he was shaken, he was not as traumatized by Steve's murder as the rest of us and was capable of dealing with my emotions and handling situations too demanding for me to manage by myself.

The day after I was told about the murder, I wanted to see where Steve had died. Gunshot Fire Road was only a two-or-three-minute drive from where we were living. Roger offered to take me. When we arrived at the trailhead, there were reporters, photographers,

TV camera teams, and news vans with satellite dishes all waiting for me, guessing that sooner or later, I would come to the site where my husband had been murdered.

From the moment Steve's name had been released some 18 hours after the murder, reporters from local and national TV stations and other media outfits had knocked on the door. They had lined up their mobile units in front of the house and along the road and had stood outside in small groups with their microphones and cameras ready, all waiting to catch a glimpse of me.

Paul had been busy answering the door and finally hired a private security firm to shield us from the media's glare and seal off, with the permission of his neighbors, the private road along which their homes were located. To help the press, Paul and Mary Alice had given a short statement on my behalf that had been shown on many TV stations.

Two security guards accompanied Roger and me. As I walked toward the trailhead, a well-known American TV presenter called out to us, "I want to do an interview with the widow!" Right. Of course. Me, with cancer and a bald head, displaying my intense grief and shock over my murdered husband on prime-time US television. The boost in advertising revenue would be staggering.

Everybody wanted the story. Everybody wanted to see the desperate, 95-pound, cancer-stricken, bald-headed, grieving widow. A sensation!

Roger guided me through the entrance to the trail, while the security guards carefully motioned the throng of journalists away, shouting, "Please move back! Give her some space!"

Steve had been coming to the end of his walk with Coco when he was killed. We soon reached the spot, while the reporters stayed behind the gate. One could see the murder location from the entrance, so the TV cameras got some footage of me, this slight, white-clad figure standing at the spot where her husband had been murdered.

I kneeled in the dirt in the exact spot where Steve was shot. His blood was still there. The dust and the little rocks were spattered with it, and there was blood on nearby weeds. I just sat there, dumbstruck and empty.

As a meditator, I knew that emptiness could be a doorway to deeper states of being, but no, not in this case. This emptiness was different. There was nothing in me. There were no emotions. It was like I myself had died.

Crying at least would have provided some kind of release instead of being dead to the world, sitting in the blood of my dead husband.

Roger recited lines from the Tibetan Phowa Ceremony, a Buddhist meditation practice performed after a loved one leaves their body. His voice resonated calm and deep, washing over me in my numbed state. I was so grateful to him because I couldn't do anything. I couldn't read anything, I couldn't say anything, I couldn't think anything.

I picked up a little rock seeped in Steve's blood and took it home with me. I still have it, safe in a small box in my nightstand drawer. When I die, it shall go with me into the flames.

CHAPTER 7

INTO THE FIRE

It was a cool and quiet morning. The sun peeked through the fog. I was alone. Roger had driven me to the trail. He would wait in the car.

I opened the door, shivered, pulled my woolly coat tight around my hunched shoulders, then slowly stumbled along the dusty trail. To the left sloped a gentle hillside covered with dried-up grass dotted with small shrubs and weeds. To the right were bay trees, oaks, and madrone bushes.

The setting was so peaceful it was impossible to believe that a cold-blooded murder had happened here just a few days before.

At the spot where Steve had died, mourners from the local community had placed flowers, messages, and mementos, creating a beautiful and touching shrine.

Shaken, lonely, and bereaved, I sat down in the dirt. My physical body was extremely weak, and my reservoir of tears had been spent.

Here was the only place where I was able to eat. My appetite, already diminished by chemotherapy, had completely vanished, and regular meals stopped.

From my small bag, I took out an energy-packed protein drink recommended for cancer patients and a banana. I forced myself to swallow the thick liquid and slowly, bite by bite, the awful-tasting banana. I hated it, but I had to eat. It was the only way to get through this nightmare.

"One bite for Steve." Slowly chewing. Swallowing. My face wet with tears.

"One bite for Coco." My mouth was filled with a disgusting taste. Chew, swallow.

"One bite for Wiebke." The banana was mushy and bitter, and the furry texture made me retch. Chew, swallow. Swallow again.

"One bite for Bebe." And on it went. That was the only way I could finish a whole banana – like a reluctant child who does not want to eat what is good for her. I was helpless and missed Steve beyond description.

After eating, I meditated silently, praying for Steve's peaceful release from his body, despite the violence he had experienced. Even though his body was lying in a police morgue, I could sense his disembodied presence lingering around the place where he died.

One day, as I was sitting there, his voice spoke to me. It was unmistakably Steve, and he told me two things I'll never forget.

He said, "Lokita, you should no longer stay in San Geronimo. You're desperately unhappy there. You need to live somewhere else."

He was right. Even though Paul and Mary Alice had been wonderful to me, their home would always remind me of Steve, of the time we spent there together, of our last night together and the conversation we had, and especially the following night when I woke in the early hours to find that Steve hadn't come home. From now on, his side of our bed would always be empty.

I had to find somewhere new to live.

The other thing Steve said to me was, "Go back to Costa Rica when you're better and enjoy everything we've created there."

I took these two messages into my heart and, with the help of my friends, set about finding a rental house in Marin. Unfortunately, my return to Costa Rica would have to wait.

The murder happened close to Spirit Rock Meditation Center in a peaceful area of natural beauty. The entire community of Marin County had been deeply shaken by what had occurred. Many people, especially those close by, expressed their wish for a special gathering on the path where Steve had been shot, in order to heal the wounds caused by the violent events.

Jack Kornfield, one of the center's founding teachers, offered to hold a ceremony for Steve, the Spirit Rock community, our family and friends, and those living in the area and beyond. Jack, author of many bestselling books on Buddhism, had trained as a Buddhist monk in the monasteries of Thailand, India, and Burma and had met Steve personally.

It was impossible for me to attend. The gathering of so many people grieving together would be too much for me. I could barely face my closest friends and knew I would be overwhelmed by everyone looking at me, wanting to offer love and heartfelt condolences. It might result in a complete emotional breakdown.

Roger and Paul told me afterwards it had been a beautiful service and that many people sent me good wishes, support, and strength.

Over the next few days, even the next few weeks, people organized prayer circles and meetings on the path, giving love and energy to Steve and blessings to the community and the surrounding nature. The shrine with flowers and messages had grown, and somebody had brought a white porcelain statue of Kuan Yin, the enlightened female bodhisattva and goddess of mercy. Others had left photos of Steve, some from years back, even before I knew him.

An autopsy had to be performed on Steve's body so that the cause of death could be used as evidence. It was unbearable not to be able to see him, but finally, on October 9th, he was brought to a nearby funeral home, and I received a call from the funeral director.

"Hello, Mrs. Carter. How are you? I'm calling to let you know that your husband's body has arrived. If you wish, you may come and see him."

I managed to squeeze a few words through my tight throat. "Thank you. Would just before noon work for you?"

Roger took me there.

We entered the ornately decorated foyer. Crystal chandeliers reflected light in a flowery pattern on the ceiling. A vase with white lilies stood on a low table by a long sofa, probably a 12-seater. The mood was somber and quiet; only the click-clack of my heels could be heard.

A man in a dark suit welcomed us at the door. He wore a name tag on his lapel, "Eddie," and it was clear that he was the funeral director. "Good morning, Mrs. Carter. Please let me express my condolences. What happened to your husband is inconceivable. I'll take care of everything for you."

Another man stood near the sofa. He took a couple of steps toward me and gently clasped both of my hands in his. "I'm the Marin County coroner. You must be Mrs. Carter. My sincerest condolences to you and your family. I'm so sorry for your shocking loss."

We sat on the sofa, and he handed me a small zip-lock bag. In it were Steve's wedding band and a necklace with a Peruvian opal, a beautiful turquoise stone, that Steve had been wearing. Steve loved that necklace and often wore it. It was touching to receive it because it held so much of Steve's energy. We had bought it together years earlier.

"It's understandable that you want to view your husband's body, Mrs. Carter. But before you do," the coroner took a deep breath, "I must warn you."

I, too, took a deep breath and braced myself for what would come next.

"Your husband was shot three times: once in the abdomen, once in the hip, and once in the lower part of his face, just above his jaw, through his cheek. There's a small plaster on his face to disguise the bullet wound, and there are bruise marks as well."

"I understand. Thank you for telling me. Now I know what to expect."

Out of nowhere, the funeral director appeared.

"Are you ready to see your husband now?"

"Yes. I'd like to be alone with him."

Eddie opened the door into a small, chapel-like room and closed it quietly behind me. I looked around slowly, taking everything in, feeling that I had entered a cool, quiet, sacred place of worship. There were rows of chairs, a large bouquet, and tall, stained-glass windows that filtered muted sunlight.

In the center of the room stood a pedestal—a trolley on wheels—on which lay a coffin-shaped box covered with a sarong, a large piece of patterned fabric that I immediately recognized. Steve and I used it many times as decoration in our workshops. One of our friends must have brought it there.

I stepped up to the coffin and saw it was made of greyish cardboard. It wasn't a wooden coffin, which puzzled me at the time, but I later learned that in California, cremations in wooden coffins had been discontinued due to environmental concerns. Cutting down trees to be burned shortly afterwards in an incinerator had never made a lot of sense to me ecologically. Yet at the time of Steve's death, a cardboard substitute didn't seem very appropriate to the gravity of this moment.

The coffin was halfway open. Steve was lying on his back, his hands folded across his stomach. He was wearing a white T-shirt.

There he was: my man, my beloved, my one and only. Dead. As the coroner had warned me, there were bruises on his face and some dried blood.

This wasn't the first time I had seen a corpse. When my mother died, I sat by her side during the final moments of her life, her death, and for some time afterwards. The doctor had told me that my mother's death was imminent, and I decided to be with her before and during the transition. I had asked her then if she wanted to practice a certain meditation with me, in which I would make an "ah" sound on each of her exhales so that we could feel connected through our breathing, as if we were one breath.

She had agreed. We inhaled together, and I sounded the "ah" at our joint exhale. After what felt like hours, I waited to inhale with her after the "ah," but there was no more inhale. Ever so gently, she had passed into the nether realms. It was a very easy and simple moment. I had always imagined there would be some dramatic scene when dying, a sharp inhale or a croaking, as is often portrayed in films. But it was as simple as her ceasing to breathe. Life and death are but a breath away from each other.

I placed petals of freesias, her favorite flowers, on her body and sat by her side, slowly coming to terms with the realization that my mother, the soul of my mother, was no longer in the body. The body was now an empty shell; like a hermit crab, she had left her shell behind.

Looking into Steve's coffin now felt similar. The body lying there was not Steve anymore. It was his body, but he was not there.

I touched his arms, which had wrapped themselves lovingly around me so many times in the past 17 years. I always loved his long, tanned arms with their soft hair and perfect muscles.

Now the arms were cold and stiff, and the tan was gone. They were gray, like the skin on his face. He had been so full of life just a few days ago, but now nothing was left of it.

I touched his hand and gently stroked his hair, but everything was lifeless. The exterior form of Steve looked utterly familiar, but whatever made him Steve, the "Steveness" of his being, was gone from his body.

Nevertheless, I made a little ceremony. On his coffin, I laid out a heart of rose petals. Inside, next to Steve's head, I placed photos of his children, me, and our dog. For a few minutes, I sat in silence with his body, mystified because his physical form was there, but Steve was not.

"May you rest in peace, my love," were my last words before I walked out of the chapel into the reception area where Eddie and Roger were waiting. We briefly discussed arrangements for the cremation service, and then Roger took me home.

The cremation took place exactly a week after Steve's murder at a facility in North Marin. We were a small group of twelve people, including my friends Bebe and Benny, Roger, Steve's family, and me.

Lauren, a mutual friend who had known and loved Steve for some 30 years, was a certified mistress of ceremonies, a wise soul, and the perfect person to conduct the service.

I brought a garland of orange-colored marigold flowers as a sign of respect and honor. This was a cultural gesture I had embraced while traveling in India and Nepal, where they use marigold garlands for weddings and other celebrations. There, these bright orange flowers represent the sun, transmitting light and positive energy, and necklaces are placed around people's necks to honor them.

My garland was also an emotional link between Steve and me. On our journey to Bhutan in 2011, we passed through Kathmandu on his birthday, and I bought a garland of marigold flowers from a vendor on the street and placed it around Steve's neck. His smile lit up the whole area.

Now, I laid the orange garland on the coffin, approximately where Steve's head and chest were lying underneath. Then everybody had the opportunity to come forward to the coffin, lay some flowers or a letter on it, and say a few words or just stand for a moment in silent tribute. The coffin was getting decorated colorfully.

Memories of our visit to Nepal passed through my mind: happy times, strong incense, strange instruments being played, and Steve's childlike wonder. He appreciated the Hindu approach to death and funeral rites. In Kathmandu, we were ambling along, exploring the alleyways and sights, when a procession of people had come dancing and singing along the street, banging drums and letting off firecrackers.

"What's happening here? What are they doing?" Steve had been curious. Coming closer, he saw that they were carrying a human corpse wrapped in a white cloth and decorated with flowers on a simple stretcher, making their way to the burning ghats, the cremation grounds.

"It's beautiful how they celebrate the departed here, so open and visible for everybody," he had commented.

A couple of days before the service, I met with Eddie at the cremation facility. First, he had shown me the chapel where the service would be held and the conveyor belt on which the casket would slowly exit through a pair of velvet curtains as the service ended. Then he had taken me out of the chapel and around the back to show me the incinerator, or furnace, where the body would be burned.

There, I made a request. "Can we avoid the part of the service where somber music is played, and the coffin slowly glides to some invisible, mysterious place beyond the curtains?" I asked. "If possible, I'd like us to guide the trolley with the casket out of the chapel. Then I would like to take it around the corner of the building and into the chamber with the incinerator alone."

Eddie looked at me in surprise. But I hadn't finished.

"Then everyone will remain outside while I go in with the coffin," I continued. "I'll remain with the coffin for a while, and then you can come and help me push it into the furnace."

Eddie hesitated.

"We don't usually do that." He frowned.

Was he wondering if I was planning on doing something drastic in the furnace room?

"Don't worry," I assured him. "I won't do anything rash."

My behavior during this time was paradoxical. On the one hand, I felt like a lifeless zombie, mechanically going through the motions of what had to be done. On the other hand, I had strong ideas of how things should be.

Eddie agreed to my requests, which was courageous because I'm sure he could have gotten into trouble if anything had gone wrong.

And so, as the cremation service ended, we wheeled Steve's coffin out of the chapel and to the corner at the back of the building, where everybody shared a final moment of goodbye.

In our workshops, Steve and I had taught the participants a ritual blessing. Everyone would rub the palms of their hands together very fast, generating heat and energy, then stretch out their arms toward a certain person—someone who was sad or who needed love—and open their palms, radiating their energy, showering the person with love.

We then did that for Steve, giving blessings to his body and his departed being. After we formed a circle around the coffin, I guided them, saying, "Now, rub your hands together, and then open them up and give love to Steve and send him off." My voice trembled. I could hardly get the words out, although I had said the same words a million times in our workshops.

Eddie and I took the trolley into the furnace room, and he then discreetly left me alone, although I suspect he was keeping an eye on me through the window.

For a few minutes, I said my final goodbyes to Steve, his body that had been his home for 67 years, and the physical form that had given me so much pleasure.

Eventually I gave Eddie a sign, and he came back in. Together, we pushed the trolley to the door of the furnace and slid the coffin inside. We closed the door, and Eddie once more left the room.

For a timeless moment, I stood looking at this peculiar scene. In a traditional funeral, where the coffin is lowered into the ground, then covered with earth, the body is still there and intact—at least for a while—as the natural process of decomposition unfolds. But here, I was going to push a button, and within a couple of hours, Steve's body would completely disappear, burned to ashes.

During a visit to India, I had witnessed the entire death ceremony. I saw the body being taken to the burning ghats, the funeral pyre, down by the river, then laid in a shallow pit, where a bed of wooden logs had been prepared, together with dried patties made from cow dung mixed with hay. The body was then covered with more wood, ghee was poured over the pyre, and relatives and friends of the deceased chanted mantras as the pyre was lit. It was all done in the open, in public view. Sometimes, if there was insufficient wood to hide it, one could even see the corpse burning. On one occasion, I heard a "pop" as the heat caused the skull to burst.

Students of Tantric traditions are asked to sit for extended periods of time in the funeral pyre grounds and meditate on impermanence and the final dissolution as a reminder that death surely will come, no matter what we do, who we are, or what we possess.

Looking through the small, round window of the furnace at the coffin, I took in this last moment with Steve, his empty shell in the coffin, acutely aware of the reality of impermanence, as taught by mystics down the ages. In the words of Gautam Buddha:

"That which is subject to origination is also subject to cessation."

That which is born has to die.

It is the *Tathata*, the suchness, the ultimate nature of all things. Something is going to happen to our bodies, to the bodies of our friends, family members, and beloveds, and to the bodies of our pets. In many cases, they will be burned. And in all cases, we have no choice but to participate in the endless cycle of birth, life, death, and renewal.

This strange and inconceivable moment of saying my last farewell was also perfectly natural because, in my acceptance and surrender, I could embrace this ultimate truth and let Steve go.

Eventually, I walked over to the wall and pressed the large green button.

It was a gas system, so I heard the burner come on with a small popping noise. For a while, there was a soft buzzing sound as the fire began to warm the inside of the furnace, and then suddenly, "Whoosh!" The chamber was filled with fire and heat.

The fire was on; the body was being burned. I had no desire to watch. Once more, I thanked Steve for everything we had shared, walked out of the room, and closed the door behind me.

Outside, I took a deep breath of fresh air and felt the warm sun on my face. At least for now, I remained in the land of the living.

Roger put his arm around me, and on the way to the car, I said, "I'm so relieved that this intense week is over." Steve had died on the evening of October 5th, I had been told about it early the next morning on October 6th, and we had the cremation ceremony on the 13th.

"I know, sweetheart. I know." Roger truly meant it. I could feel the tenderness of his heart.

"I wish I could have some alone time now, a quiet space to understand and try to integrate everything that has happened."

But it was not to be. Back at Paul and Mary Alice's house, the friends and family who had attended the ceremony had gathered for a repast—to eat, mourn, and share our sorrow over Steve's death.

On the table in the living room, Paul and Mary Alice had arranged flowers and a collection of photos of Steve. Everyone admired the photos and started telling stories of when they had been together with Steve, but I couldn't participate. I couldn't eat anything and was nowhere ready to tell stories.

All I wanted was to disappear there and then. Yet I felt obliged to stay. The gathering continued for a couple of hours until finally, I could retire to my bed.

It took me several years to be strong enough to relive happy moments with Steve and talk about him without falling apart emotionally. Sometimes I judged myself for how long it took. Lying awake at night, I wondered whether I would have grieved the loss of Steve differently had I not been going through cancer treatment when he died. Perhaps it wouldn't have taken so long. Maybe it would have been a smoother process. With patience and self-compassion, I accepted that whatever time it took was the right time for me.

There were more challenges for me to face. The day after Steve's funeral, or maybe the day after that, I had an appointment with my oncologist because the cancer treatment was continuing. Of course, Dr. Susanna knew what had happened—everybody knew.

I sat in her office and cried.

"Susanna," I said, "I don't want to continue the treatment right now. It's too much. I need a break, maybe a month, to pull myself back together." I put my face in my hands. "I simply can't continue with the treatment."

With a firm yet gentle voice, Dr. Susanna reminded me that chemotherapy has to be given in a continuous sequence. One can't stop here and there, taking breaks, and expect it to have the same effect.

"Lokita, believe me, I completely understand you're having the most horrible, challenging time right now, but let me ask you this: Do you really think you'll feel any better a month from now?"

I looked at her through the veil of my tears and thought for a moment. "No, for sure, I won't."

She gave me a sympathetic half-smile. "Well then, let's continue the treatment."

The next infusion was a couple of days later. Although I attempted to do my usual visualization of welcoming the healing elixir into my body, I spent the entire time crying.

I was crying, crying, crying. What else could I do? My beloved had just been murdered, my body was being poisoned with chemotherapy, and the line between life and death seemed perilously thin.

I was balancing like a tightrope walker between life and death. I could fall one way or the other, and I wasn't particularly bothered which way I went. It would have been quite easy for me to die, I thought.

But there were lifelines, or perhaps I should call them "heartlines," pulling me toward the living. I couldn't abandon my *doghter*, still recovering at UC Davis. She had been undergoing a series of operations, first to remove one eye, destroyed by the bullet, and then to replace the shattered part of her jaw with a fully working artificial substitute.

Knowing she had to endure all this made me want to survive so I could be there for her when she came out of the hospital. If I died, I was certain she would feel it and suffer even more than she had already.

Moreover, I couldn't abandon my family and friends, who were grieving along with me and so generously and steadfastly devoted their time, energy, and love to help me through this nightmare.

Basically, I couldn't die. Of course, if the great universe, in its infinite wisdom, had ordained my death, I would have gone anyway. But it appeared not to be part of my destiny right now.

Yes, I wanted to die, but I chose to live instead.

CHAPTER 8

A TIME OF RECKONING

My next project was to find a new place to live.

"Hello, Maureen, this is Lokita." We had once met each other years ago.

"Oh, hi, Lokita. How are you?" I was getting tired of these empty, how-are-you questions.

"Well, you probably heard about Steve's murder and that I have cancer, so I'm not doing all that good."

"Yes, I understand. My condolences."

"Thank you. I'm looking for a place to live for about six months, and I heard through the grapevine that you have a garden apartment for rent."

"Yes, I do. We can fix a time for you to come and see it. Oh, and by the way..." her voice became hesitant. "You know, Lokita, since the news broke, I've been wondering, if you don't mind me asking, who was shot first? Steve or the dog?"

I drew in a sharp breath, momentarily immobilized and speechless, then hung up. I stared into space as tears welled up in my eyes. Presumably, Maureen hadn't intended to be cruel, but her question was a stab in my heart.

I had become hypersensitive. Meeting me after Steve's murder must have been difficult and I can imagine people's helplessness in the face of such an enormous tragedy. Often, I was confronted by acquaintances with their eyes low, looking down at the floor as if searching for the right words to say. Sometimes there were platitudes like, "Everything happens for a reason," or "Everything will be okay, Lokita."

I wanted to shout, "How do you know?! Maybe Steve's murder did *not* happen for any reason other than that some stupid, mindless drug addicts needed a car and decided to kill him! And maybe things won't be okay! Maybe I'll die!"

At other times, there was pity. I could feel it immediately. A well-intentioned person might approach me with big, round, melancholy eyes, a mournful expression, and say gushingly, "Oh Lokita, I'm so, so sorry…." Then they would avoid eye contact, looking here and there, maybe searching for an escape route.

It wasn't the words themselves but how they were expressed that made me feel something was wrong with me, that I was this terribly sad, unfortunate, pitiable wretch of a human being.

At such times, I wanted to yell out, "Hey, look at me. I'm alive! Look what an amazing life we all have right now, in this very moment!" Actually, I did say this quite a few times.

Perhaps those who showed pity in this way, instead of experiencing genuine compassion, projected their misery on me as a way of feeling better about themselves, happy that they weren't in my situation.

Soon after the exchange with Maureen, I signed the lease on a furnished house with four bedrooms in the Terra Linda area of San Rafael, ideally located within a short distance of the cancer center, the hospital, and my friends. Generous donations to the GoFundMe campaign meant I could afford to rent it.

It was too big for me to live there alone. I would have been too lonely, and I couldn't function by myself. I needed a caretaker because I was so weak and sick from the cancer treatment, not to mention grieving.

Roger, who had already done so much for me, would have been an ideal housemate. But he needed to put his own life back together after his home burned down in the Valley Fire. Besides that, Tinkerbell, his beloved cat, was waiting for him in Middletown.

However, another friend, Logan, had also been affected by the Valley Fire. I knew he was looking for a way to leave Middletown temporarily until he figured out how to revive his Harbin-based business. Over the years, Steve and I forged a close connection with him. He had been our office manager, organizer, and sometimes business advisor. More than that, I intuitively knew that Logan and I were from the same tribe.

"Hi Logan, how are you?" I said when he answered the phone.

"Oh, you know, it's been very challenging. Harbin is gone, and I'm feeling like a boat adrift on the ocean. And you?"

"Ah well, I'm doing okay, given the circumstances. I miss Steve so much. Now I've moved into a new place in Terra Linda, and it's very empty," I explained. "Also, I'm looking for a support person who can help me during my cancer treatment. Driving me to treatments and so forth."

"Yes, I miss Steve, too." He sounded wistful. "What kind of person are you thinking about as your caretaker? Would they live in the house with you?"

"Well, I'm looking for someone like you—a trusted friend, a kindred spirit, and someone who needs a home. I'm wondering if you might be interested?"

I could hear Logan give a little gasp of surprise. "Well," he replied hesitantly, "I'm excited by the possibility. Let me mull it over and get back to you tomorrow."

We talked about a few more logistics and hung up.

The next day he called me and said yes. Logan moved in a couple of days later and became my primary caretaker. The house filled up with life.

Logan was the one who drove me to most of my treatment appointments, helped me with preparing meals, and sat by my side on the cold tile floor when my head was over the toilet bowl and I was vomiting from chemotherapy. He held me close when I was wailing with the pain of losing Steve, watched silly soap operas on TV with me, and entertained me with gossip and stories.

The layout of the house was perfect for sharing. Upstairs was a master suite with a bedroom, a small sitting room that could double as a dressing room, a bathroom complete with a bathtub, and three smaller bedrooms with their shared bathroom. I moved into the master suite and Logan used two rooms, one for his office and one for his bedroom, while the remaining room remained open for guests.

At first, I was a little apprehensive about living upstairs because I was very weak and couldn't climb stairs all that well, but fortunately, the staircase had a wall on one side and a railing on the other so I could support myself going up and down.

Downstairs was a large, open-plan living room with a casual dining area opening out to a walled-in private garden, plus a modern open kitchen with all the amenities, a formal dining area with a large table and eight chairs, and a guest bathroom. There was an entry hall from which one could access the three-car garage with laundry facilities.

On a table across from the front door, I created a sacred space in Steve's memory with several photos of him, a Buddha statue, Steve's Peruvian opal necklace, and fresh flowers. Steve's good friend Allen brought a large yellow orchid that continued to bloom on the altar the entire seven months I stayed there.

Friends came to see me, bringing food, taking Coco for long walks after we were reunited, keeping me company in the garden, enjoying the sunshine, and comforting me when I was desperate. Most of the time, they would stay for about half an hour, the maximum time I could manage before I became exhausted and would need to lie down.

Bebe would often sit with me during meals, bringing me up to speed with all the news and local gossip, or take me for slow, short walks in the nearby park. Mary Alice lent me her recumbent stationary bike so that I could get some gentle exercise at home. Margot offered her large, precious amethyst crystal to place below Steve's altar to support healing. I remember Paul helping me through a particularly rough tidal wave of grief, an intense, cathartic hour of screaming, crying, and expressing the horror of what was happening to me.

All my friends from near and far were incredibly supportive—I could write an entire book just about that. They reminded me, each in their own way, that life can be good, that I'm so loved, and that I could come back from this cliff of despair.

Then one day, there was a ray of light amid the dark clouds. Cindy from the Marin Humane Society called to say it would now be okay for me to visit Coco. She volunteered to drive me there.

After lunch, Cindy picked me up.

So far, I had only spoken to Cindy on the phone. When I met her in person, she struck me as a no-nonsense, bighearted, outdoorsy woman with endless energy. She was kind and conveyed the emotional power she poured into her chosen vocation of saving and protecting animals.

"Oh, Lokita, it's so good to finally meet you." She put her arms around me and pulled me close to her heart. I liked her immediately. On the way to UC Davis, she updated me on Coco's treatment. "You already know that Coco lost her right eye. She also had several operations on her jaw. We work with an excellent canine surgeon who specializes in dental surgery for dogs. Given what she's been through, Coco is doing quite well."

According to Cindy, Coco had become the most beloved dog in the animal clinic. "She is so sweet-natured, well-behaved, and laid back! The clinic team allows her to sit under their desks at work. They take her on their lunch breaks, so Coco doesn't have to lie all by herself in a kennel."

Coco's medical care was expensive. I certainly couldn't afford it, but Cindy had assured me early on that the Marin Humane Society would pay for everything.

The drive took just over an endless hour, but we finally arrived at the entrance hall to the veterinary clinic at UC Davis.

"Hello Cindy. Hello Mrs. Carter. Please wait outside for a moment while we fetch Coco for you," said the receptionist.

I was both nervous and excited to see my dog again. My heart was racing. What would her reaction be?

"Oh, Cindy, I don't know," I said. All of a sudden, I was full of doubt. "Maybe Coco wants to see Steve, not me. Maybe she won't recognize me because I look so different with all my hair gone!"

Come to think of it, I probably smelled different, too.

"I don't think she'll have any expectations." Cindy gently put her hand on my arm and looked at me.

At that moment, the veterinary team arrived with Coco on the leash. As soon as she came through the door, she immediately recognized me and pulled hard on the leash to jump into my arms.

"Coco, oh my Cocoli, I missed you so much!" I cried out as I crouched down to her level.

"I missed you so, so much, my doggie; you're the best dog!" I said through the rivers of tears now flowing down my cheeks. Coco was jumping up with her forelegs to touch my face and shoulders, toppling me over. Then we were cuddling on the floor. We must have looked a strange pair, Coco with her one eye and swollen face and skinny me with my bald head!

From the corner of my eyes, I could see that by now, the veterinary team was surrounding us, sharing the happiness of our reunion, crying tears of joy, and clapping their hands. This was the moment they had been anticipating, and it couldn't have been any sweeter. I knew then, at the core of my being, that Coco wasn't just Steve's dog. She was my dog, too, and I was her human.

Our reunion was short, but with time enough to see Coco brimming over with life, pulling on the leash and ready to chase a nearby squirrel up a tree.

She wasn't coming home with me that day. We would have to wait a few more weeks until her recovery was complete, and I was emotionally and physically strong enough to take care of her. With full hearts, Cindy and I drove back to Terra Linda.

In the meantime, preparations were in progress for an initial hearing of the trio accused of killing Steve. They were due to be arraigned, and on October 20th, 15 days after Steve's killing, I was invited to a preparatory meeting at the district attorney's office at the Marin County Civic Center to talk with the prosecutors. Lauren, our friend who had conducted the cremation service, came with me.

Marin County's Civic Center is huge. It was designed in the late 1950s by Frank Lloyd Wright, the futuristic architect, and constructed in the early 1960s, shortly after Wright's death. Its pink stucco walls, blue roof, and scalloped balconies are famous, and the number of offices along the endless hallway inside seemed uncountable—honestly, it felt like we walked past ten thousand doors looking for the DA's department.

As we finally entered the office, a distinguished-looking man in his sixties came forward to greet me.

"Hello, Mrs. Carter. Thank you for coming," he said. "I'm Ed Berberian, District Attorney for Marin County."

Ed was tall, his handshake warm and reassuring. His voice exuded wisdom. He had an almost fatherly appearance and a strong manly presence that felt safe and relaxing.

I was in awe of meeting him in person, but he soon explained that he wouldn't be handling the case himself because he was shortly due to retire, having worked in the Marin District Attorney's office for 42 years.

Instead, he introduced me to two of his deputy district attorneys, Leon Kousharian and Aicha Mievis, who would be prosecuting this case together and whom I would get to know well over the coming months.

With his broad shoulders and height, Leon was an impressive man. Soft-spoken and strong at the same time, he emanated integrity and determination. The difficult circumstances under which we were compelled to meet forged an authentic connection between Leon and me that later developed into a lasting friendship.

His prosecution partner, Aicha, was an attractive woman in her late thirties who lit up the room with her intelligence and natural elegance. We shook hands, and as I looked into her sparkling brown eyes, I saw a vibrant, vivacious, and determined woman with a huge heart. Once she started speaking, I knew she was dedicated passionately to her work and committed to supporting me throughout the unfathomable court process. We became good friends and continue to stay in contact to this day.

"We've all been shaken by this terrible crime and your personal health difficulties," Ed told me. "The three people accused of killing Steve were transferred from Portland to Marin and are now in custody here in the county jail, in this building, awaiting trial."

"In this building" were the three words I heard the loudest. I was in the same building as my beloved's murderers. The knot in my throat tightened some more.

The purpose of the meeting, he added, was to decide how best to proceed with the prosecution and what penalties should be requested from the court, which was why he had also invited several police officers involved in the case.

There was a long list of charges, the most important being the charge of first-degree murder, for which the penalty could be either life in prison without the possibility of parole or the death penalty.

I was asked for my opinion. "I have never been in favor of the death penalty. Too many people were executed, only to be found innocent later," I said.

However, in this case, there was no doubt that the three accused were guilty of the crime. They senselessly murdered two innocent people, and there was plenty of evidence to convict them.

During the meeting, it emerged that those on death row often receive superior treatment. They get better legal representation, more privileges, and more respect from their fellow prisoners.

Someone in the room pointed out that although hundreds of people—mostly men but also a few women—were given the death sentence in California during the past couple of decades, there had been no actual executions since 2006.

I preferred the life sentence over the death penalty. Steve's killers should live to face the consequences of their actions and receive the same treatment as all the other prisoners.

This wasn't an easy meeting. It might sound as if we all just sat down and discussed these issues in a matter-of-fact way, but there were many overwhelming moments when tears, pain, anger, despair—the whole range of emotions—welled up amid the talk.

When the meeting was over, Lauren and I walked out of the building and talked for a moment.

"Well done, Lokita. I'm proud you managed to get through the meeting in one piece!"

"Thanks for coming, Lauren. Thank you for your support." We hugged.

"I like the two deputy district attorneys, Leon and Aicha," Lauren added. "They make a good team. For sure, they'll get a conviction that'll put the suspects behind bars for a long time."

Yes, I wanted them to rot in jail. I wanted them to suffer for years and have an endless amount of time to think about what they did and how they destroyed their lives.

Steve's family also had direct contact with the prosecution team, and we all agreed on the prosecution strategy.

My family in Europe was deeply worried about me, but my elderly father was too fragile to fly to California. At the same time, my sister Wiebke could not take time off work at short notice and had two young children to care for. However, Wiebke's husband, my brother-in-law Gerhard, flew to be with me, arriving a couple of days after the meeting with the district attorneys.

Gerhard was a Danish farmer, one year younger than me, with a sensitive nature and a great sense of humor. He hadn't left his homeland much, feeling most comfortable on the land in Southern Denmark.

The first time I met him was at our family wedding ceremony in October 1999. It had been his first trip to the United States, and his suitcase hadn't arrived, so I had to introduce him to huge, American-style shopping malls and department stores, buying essential clothing and renting a tuxedo for the ceremony.

For Gerhard, leaving Denmark was like being a fish out of water, so for him to drop everything now and travel all the way to California, barely two weeks after Steve died, was a selfless gesture.

He and Steve had enjoyed each other a lot, and his death tore Gerhard up emotionally. He was willing to be a supportive male presence by my side at the first court hearing.

The initial hearing was scheduled for October 29th. Its purpose was to establish whether the three accused had acquired legal representation through the county's public defenders' office because none had the financial means to hire a lawyer.

Leon advised me that I could attend the hearing, sit in the courtroom, and see the defendants. Gerhard could also come in, not only to support me but for his own sake. He was hoping that by encountering the killers, he could at least begin to resolve his anger and grief and accept what had happened. In Denmark, shootings like this were almost nonexistent, whereas in the United States, they occurred almost daily.

At the Marin Civic Center Gerhard and I were ushered into a room adjoining the court where the prosecutors and police officers were waiting.

Then came the moment. "It's time to go in, Lokita."

The walls closed in on me. I couldn't do it. I couldn't bear to look at Steve's killers. It was impossible.

Gerhard went with Leon and Aicha while I stayed behind with my liaison officer. This sympathetic woman was looking after me under the State's policy of providing care for victims of violent crime. She held my hand during the entire hearing.

The murderers were right next door. There was only a thin wall between them and me.

Emotionally, I was there, inside the courtroom. My heart was being ripped to shreds, and the thought struck me, *this is really happening.*

The situation had a surreal quality. It was like sitting at home, watching a television crime series like *NYPD Blue* or *LA Law*, and then suddenly finding myself *inside* the drama. For a moment, I didn't know anymore. Was this real, or was it a TV show? Is this my reality, or is it just a bad dream?

The hearing concluded, and Gerhard returned to the room, looking distraught. We said our goodbyes to the prosecutors, left the building, and drove home.

Those were grim days, not made easier by the new course of chemotherapy I was receiving every week. In the beginning, it seemed milder than the Red Devil, with fewer side effects. But soon my feet started swelling, my toes went dark red and the skin hard, my hands thickened, and my nails turned black. Eventually, I had to discontinue the 12-week program halfway through.

Once again, I faced the reality of having little to no control over my life and body or, indeed, whether I lived or died. Nothing ever happens according to schedule during any planned course of treatment for cancer. Side effects are unique to each patient.

This was a time to practice patience and acceptance even more than earlier in the process. My goal had been to complete the 12 infusions, get the operation, get through the radiation, and be done. It wasn't working out that way.

Gerhard and I arrived at the funeral home the day after the court hearing to collect Steve's ashes. Eddie greeted us at the entrance with a cheerful smile and a smooth, professional manner.

"Good morning, Mrs. Carter. How are you today?"

To my sensitive nerves, his mechanical greeting felt phony and out of place, especially given the gravity of the occasion.

"What kind of a question is that?" I lashed out at Eddie. "How do you think I feel? I'm here to pick up my murdered husband's ashes. Why do you even bother to ask?"

Eddie inhaled sharply and stared at me for a moment, his eyes wide open. I continued, "Please, let's be real here. This is a very hard moment for me."

It wasn't fair to Eddie. My emotional reaction contained so much more pain and anguish than his greeting had caused. I was about as miserable as a human being can be.

Eddie surprised me. As we sat down in his office, he apologized. "I'm so sorry, Mrs. Carter. Forgive me. I was on autopilot. I didn't even think how you might be feeling. I should've been more sensitive."

His sincerity touched me, and I felt humbled and embarrassed by my behavior. "I'm also sorry. It's just so incredibly difficult," I tried to apologize. "I'm probably not the only person who makes a scene in your funeral home. Death is so difficult for all."

In death, we have to let go of family and friends forever. Some people find solace in their faith, some in their spiritual practice, and others comfort themselves with aphorisms like "this too shall pass," "time heals all wounds," or "she is in a better place now." Regardless, every day gives us the opportunity to look inside ourselves and cultivate that within us which will not die when we leave the body.

Eddie presented Gerhard and me with a brown, no-frills, rectangular plastic box about 12 inches high containing Steve's ashes.

"Of course, you can purchase a different kind of urn if you'd like something more elegant." Eddie handed me a brochure showing various models made of wood, ceramic, brass, or bronze, and their prices.

I shook my head. "The plastic box is fine," I told him, "but I have a special request."

Usually, after a cremation, the remains are sealed in an urn, just as Eddie had done. In a ceremony, the urn is placed in a location that the deceased may have indicated, or the relatives decide. This could be a cemetery, a memorial home, a family house, a bedside table, or a garden. The possibilities are endless.

Every time Steve and I had discussed death and what kind of arrangements we would like for our funerals and mortal remains, he had shown stubborn resistance to going into detail.

"It's very simple. I want my body to be burned, and I don't want my ashes to be buried in my hometown, Madera."

He refused to give any further instructions, saying, "Ah well, who knows what's going to happen anyway? We'll figure it out later. There's plenty of time!"

So, I was in a quandary. On my way to pick up Steve's ashes, I had come to a decision. "Basically, Steve's ashes need to be divided into three: one for his children, one for his brothers, and one for me."

Eddie looked shocked. "This is a highly unusual request," he objected, scratching his head.

"This is a highly unusual situation," I replied.

I must have been one of Eddie's more problematic clients. First, I had redesigned the cremation ceremony, then I had been rude to him, and now this. But Eddie had a good heart, with a courageous and flexible attitude to his vocation.

"Well, let me see what I can do," he said, finally. I handed him the three ornately embroidered velvet pouches I had brought. Then he picked up the urn and disappeared into a side room. After a while, he returned with the pouches, the ashes evenly divided between them.

He placed them in Gerhard's open hands with great respect and reverence. It was a deeply touching moment, and I thanked Eddie from the bottom of my heart. All three of us had tears in our eyes as we said goodbye.

In the end, there were three ceremonies held for Steve. Sadly, because of my ill health, I couldn't participate in the ones held by his family. As for my ceremony, I decided to wait until I returned to Costa Rica.

Gerhard was with me for five days, giving me a precious respite from the intense whirlwind of cancer treatment and courtroom drama. On one of those days, he wanted to go shopping because, for people from Europe, everything in the US is so much cheaper. Since retail therapy worked well for me, we took the ferry from Marin to downtown San Francisco.

It was a cold, sunny day in early fall, and my brother-in-law and I stood close together on the ship's deck, wrapped up in warm coats, admiring the Golden Gate Bridge and the view of the Bay Area cities as we cruised past Alcatraz toward the piers. I deeply appreciated Gerhard's comforting presence and solid sense of family and love, so much so that tears of gratitude started rolling down my cheeks. Looking back at the ordeal of that year, this is one of the moments that stands out in its power and beauty.

Three weeks after Steve died, another beam of sunshine in those dark times was the first meeting with my therapist. My liaison officer had informed me that the State of California had a budget for victims of violent crime and would pay for intensive psychotherapy for me to help integrate and heal everything I had been through.

It was important for me to find someone who understood trauma healing and my background in meditation and spiritual growth. On impulse, I called the Spirit Rock Meditation Center. They referred me to Dr. Matt Spalding, assuring me he had the qualities and experience I was looking for.

Dr. Spalding and I spoke on the phone, and I soon found myself warming to his friendly, calm manner. I booked an appointment with him at his office in Fairfax for the next day.

On the wall of Dr. Spalding's office was a Buddhist *tangka* painting showing a Buddha-like figure sitting in deep meditation on a lotus flower. A bright oriental rug lay on the floor, dark red cushions of various sizes were scattered around the room, and small wooden tables with ornate inlays stood on each side of a dark orange velvet sofa. The atmosphere was like that of a small, peaceful temple.

Dr. Spalding appeared and walked toward me with an outstretched hand and a warm smile. He looked quite formal in his grey pants and white dress shirt, especially in this otherwise very colorful environment. Looking at him, I knew he was the right therapist for me. I felt at home.

He invited me to sit on the sofa across from where he took his seat in a comfortable armchair.

"Thank you for coming today. Please feel free to call me Matt," he introduced himself and then asked softly, looking into my eyes, "How are you feeling, Lokita?"

I had no words. Nothing, absolutely nothing, could describe the way I felt. Immediately, I burst into tears. My life had come to a point where crying was a regular, almost permanent thing, and by now, the tears didn't simply run down my cheeks like normal tears. No, they sprang out of my eyes at a ninety-degree angle.

Eventually, the tears subsided, and he listened attentively as I reeled off the details of my situation. When I had finished, he assured me, "Everything you're going through, Lokita, I can feel with you, and I'm here for you. We will do this together. We will form a relationship, you and I, where you can tell me everything and be whoever you are, with your feelings, with everything you have: your grief, your anger, your shock, and your desperation. You can bring everything to me."

I knew in my heart of hearts that this was true. In our six-year, therapeutic relationship, we had many sessions—face-to-face while I was in California and later online when either of us travelled. Coco was welcome and sat by my side during many of the sessions after we had been reunited.

Dr. Matt possessed the perfect combination of psychotherapy experience and a rich spiritual history. Like in the Tantric tradition, his premise was that we are fundamentally enlightened and perfect human beings. Rather than seeking out what was wrong with me and trying to fix it, he focused on the divine light within me, which was somehow unaffected by external circumstances, however dim it may have been.

Dr. Matt listened to me with an open heart, interest, and profound presence. He never gave superficial advice. Instead, he reached beyond traditional psychology into the realm of spiritual teachings. For example, to illustrate a particular point, he would tell a story about what the eighth-century Buddhist mystic Rinpoche Padmasambhava did in Tibet or what Gautam Siddhartha said to his chief disciple Ananda.

At times, my grief and pain were so overwhelming that all I could do was sink into a dark hole of despair, sobbing, wailing, and forgetting everything around me. My world had come to a halt. How was it possible that the actual world, the so-called "real" world, was continuing? The sun was still rising, the birds were still singing, and people went about their business every day as if nothing significant had happened.

Dr. Matt's stories brought me into the here and now, into the present moment, as I sat on the sofa across from him. My feelings of sorrow were still there, but the stories gave me a broader perspective and helped me regain my inner strength.

In these moments, rather than being tossed around in tidal waves of emotions, I could free myself from the drama of the tragedy that had befallen me and look at it as a witness—detached and observing.

As a *Tantrika*, someone who practices Tantric meditation, deep down, I knew that true equanimity, the middle path, would help me get through this period of my life. There would always be grief and pain. Yet there would also be joy and blissfulness. Walking the middle path, I could see that they belonged together, and like rain and sunshine, they were two sides of the same coin.

CHAPTER 9

FACING THE ACCUSED

"**H**ablas español?"

The question was relevant because, by nature, I'm not a moody or depressed person. Despite all the challenges and heartache, I felt a spark of life saying, "Lokita, find something fun to do, something that feels good and uplifting."

Since I intended to return to Costa Rica eventually, working on my Spanish seemed a great way to bring a little normalcy back into my shattered life.

Online, I discovered a Spanish school in downtown San Rafael. Felipe, the owner and lead teacher, invited me to meet with him to check which level of Spanish class I could join.

Felipe was Colombian-American and welcomed me warmly. We chatted away in Spanish as best as I could so he could assess my level of linguistic skill. He turned out to be an excellent teacher, assigning me to an intermediate class meeting twice a week.

There were about fifteen people in the room when I arrived for my first class, and I was nervous, despite being accustomed to leading workshops, sometimes with hundreds of people. It's always challenging to be the new kid on the block when everyone else already knows each other. Never mind my bald head and gaunt appearance!

"Hola, Lokita, bienvenido a nuestra clase. Please take any free seat." Everybody looked at me expectantly.

"Would you like to introduce yourself?" I wasn't sure whether I should do that in English or Spanish, but since I wanted to avoid blushing, I took the easier route.

"Okay, I'm Lokita. I live in Costa Rica and am in Marin County for cancer treatment. I'd like to improve my Spanish."

They all welcomed me in Spanish. Then someone asked, "Are you married? Do you have a partner?"

That was the wrong thing to ask. Tears immediately sprang from my eyes. There I was, in a room full of strangers, crying my eyes out, telling them that my husband was the one who had been murdered a few weeks earlier in Fairfax.

But it was also the right thing to ask because everybody knew the story, and sooner or later, it would have had to come out. The room was full of condolences and compassion.

One woman took me aside after class. "I work for the San Rafael Sheriff's Office as the police psychologist," she confided. "I supported the officers who were the first to arrive at the scene of your husband's murder. They were so shaken when they found his body lying on the trail, his lifeless hand still holding Coco on the leash."

What a small world, I thought, as my heart went out to the police officers. This was the first time I thought about what they must have felt. Tears of compassion flowed down my cheeks.

She squeezed my hand in a tender gesture of support. "Everybody is rooting for you and your dog, Lokita."

Once we had cleared the initial hurdle of my sensational story, I was accepted as just another classmate. Everyone got the point. I was there to learn Spanish and focus my mind on something ordinary and practical rather than on chemotherapy, the loss of my beloved husband, and the looming homicide case.

I enjoyed those classes. They were relaxing, and I could laugh, make mistakes, be silly with my Spanish, feel like a schoolgirl, and forget for a moment the nightmares outside. They were good times, providing rays of sunshine amid the heavy storm clouds surrounding me.

One oddity the rest of the class enjoyed about me was that whenever Felipe asked me a question in Spanish, I automatically started to reply in German, my mother tongue. I probably wouldn't have noticed if my classmates hadn't laughed out loud. We all marveled at the complexity of the human brain. When I finally returned to Costa Rica, my Spanish was much better, and I sounded more like a teenager than a toddler.

All the while, my thoughts circled the murder trial and my participation in the courtroom drama. Those affected by a crime have the right to share with the court the emotional, financial, and physical impact the crime had on them. While in my mind, Steve and Audrey were the victims because they lost their lives, from the court's perspective, the immediate family was considered the ultimate victims.

Usually, so-called victim impact statements are delivered at the end of a trial, when the judge has heard all the evidence, received either a guilty plea from the defendant or a guilty verdict from the jury, and is ready to pronounce the sentence.

In our case, such statements could be made by me, Steve's children, and the family of Audrey, the young woman who was killed in Golden Gate Park by the same three suspects.

However, I was very ill, and nobody could say when the sentencing of Steve's killers was going to happen. It was unclear when, or indeed if, there would be a trial. The wheels of justice turn slowly, and due process takes time, especially in a murder trial where the death penalty might be imposed.

I shared my concerns with Leon and Aicha. "I don't know if I'll still be alive when it's time to stand up in court and make my impact statement. I'd feel better if I did something about it now because I may die soon. But I want the court and those three killers to know how their actions have impacted me."

The prosecutors were sympathetic.

"Normally, it's not done," advised Leon. "Normally, the statement is declared to the court verbally by the person involved or read aloud by a lawyer."

"But under these circumstances, let's make a video," Aicha chimed in. "We can ask the judge's permission to present it at court."

We decided to tape it at home in Terra Linda. On the morning of the filming, Leon and Aicha were there, plus a couple of supportive friends and the camera team.

I sat in front of Steve's altar, where there was a photo of him, my pouch with his ashes, and some flowers. I wore a dark sweater and looked pale and gaunt, with no makeup, my shaved head exposed, and a pair of reading glasses on my nose in case I needed prompting from the script I had written the evening before.

The recording began, and I introduced myself as Steve's wife, explained that we had been happily together for 17 years, then talked about our retirement to Costa Rica, the discovery of breast cancer, and our decision to return to California for treatment.

I described the events of October 5th and the loss of my beloved husband, including being robbed of his support as my primary caretaker during the cancer treatment.

"As you can imagine, I'm devastated by this incomprehensible act," I continued. "My whole life is in crisis and filled with despair and hopelessness."

Recording this video was particularly poignant since I had to imagine that I was addressing the court and the people who killed Steve, and because I knew this video might be shown after my death.

While I spoke, I could hear sobbing and the rustle of paper tissues being passed around.

Finally, it was over. A heavy load was off my shoulders. Now I didn't need to worry that my death would prevent me from sharing my situation with the court. Steve's killers would see me and be confronted with the impact of their crime.

After the recording team had packed up and everybody had left, it was time to drive to the airport to pick up my sister Wiebke, who was coming to stay with me for two weeks. Her husband Gerhard had flown back to Denmark and was looking after their two children, aged twelve and six, allowing Wiebke to be with me. Tears flowed as we held each other close.

While growing up in Germany, Wiebke and I hadn't been particularly close. The five-year age gap had been too wide for us to bond easily as teenagers, but as adults, we found we had more and more in common, with a steadily growing affection for each other. Her sense of humor is identical to mine. We can laugh about the same things, and we easily understand each other. In some ways, we are quite different; in others, very alike. We do look different. Wiebke has my mother's brown eyes and hair, whereas I tend more toward my father's side of the family, with blue eyes and blond hair.

A couple of days after Wiebke's arrival, the trio accused of killing Steve was scheduled to appear in court to hear the charges and enter their pleas. Wiebke had known this ahead of time and was determined to be by my side as we faced them together.

In the media, there have been reports about cases in which the murderers were never found and arrested and that the family and loved ones of the murder victim couldn't find peace and move forward with their lives. In our case, I found consolation in the fact that the suspects were in jail, there was a car filled with evidence and a gun, and I could put faces on Steve's killers rather than despairing about an unknown assailant on the loose.

On the way to the Marin Civic Center, Wiebke grew concerned about me. "How do you feel?" She could see that I was tapping my foot on the car's floor.

"Actually, I'm nervous about what will happen in the courtroom. I'm afraid I'll fall apart in front of the killers."

"I'm your sister and here to help you. We can do this together!"

We made our way through the labyrinth, passing through countless hallways and past many doors until we arrived at the courtroom entrance. Leon and the prosecution team were waiting and greeted us warmly. In the few minutes before going in, I shared my feelings with Leon.

"I don't know how I'm going to be able to control myself when I see those people," I admitted. "I may want to jump across the courtroom barrier and hit them. Or at least scream at them."

Leon took my statement very seriously. "Whatever you want to do, Lokita, I totally understand, but you must not do that," he warned me. "You may damage our prosecution effort, and most certainly, you will be removed from the courtroom.

"Force yourself to sit on that chair," he added. "You'll manage, you can do it, you are a woman of incredible strength."

Wiebke and I entered the courtroom and sat in the first row, right behind where the suspects would soon take their seats.

Again, I found myself wondering, "Is this real? Or am I dreaming?"

In some strange way, I could see the illusory nature of the contracts we all make with each other—agreements to think in a certain way, to act in a certain way—and thereby create the social order in which we live, with its rules, laws, and punishments.

There is a famous quote by Gautam Buddha: "We are what we think, all that we are arises with our thoughts, with our thoughts we make the world." From this perspective, the courts and criminal code were here only because we had thought them into existence.

Although the hearing was open to the public, Wiebke and I were the only audience. Along the back wall stood a line of tall and solid-looking police officers, clearly ready to pounce and defend if necessary.

In front of us, to our left, were the prosecutors, Aicha and Leon. To the right were the attorneys representing the accused. An official recorder sat to one side in front of the judge's bench.

Then, a side door opened, and the three suspects were brought into the room. They wore prison suits with broad red and white stripes, were shackled with chains at their feet, and had their hands cuffed behind their backs. An air of eeriness filled the courtroom.

The sound of the chains rattling was a potent reminder of the seriousness of the situation. The police and custodian officials weren't taking any chances.

According to the press, they were drifters, homeless people who lived on the street. They were dirty-looking and scruffy with pasty complexions and shaved heads because their hair had been riddled with lice when they were arrested.

The prosecution team had told me that the trio had been high on crystal meth during their killing spree, and now they had the drained, weary look of addicts being forced to go cold turkey.

I recognized each of the defendants from photos shown to me by Leon and Aicha and from numerous posts on online media. Nearest to me sat Sean Angold, aged 23, who had allegedly stolen the gun from a car in San Francisco. In the middle was Lila Alligood, 18, who was said to have chosen Steve as their target while they were waiting on the path near Fairfax for someone to rob. Furthest away from me was Morrison Lampley, 23, who was thought to be the one who pulled the trigger.

Alligood was reported to have been Lampley's longtime girlfriend, while their association with Angold was said to be relatively recent.

Wiebke reached over and took my hand. Hers was clammy and cold, and I didn't dare to look at her because meeting her eyes would have pushed me right over the edge. My throat was constricted, and I wanted to scream out in anger, pain, and disgust or do something irrational.

I focused on my breathing, keeping it slow and deep, forcing myself to stay calm and not give in to the adrenaline rushing through my bloodstream, ready for an emotional outburst.

"This is a very serious moment, so let the court take its time and do things properly," I told myself. "Stay calm, Lokita. You may not live long enough to see these people again."

My only role was to sit and be a silent witness to this spectacle. I reminded myself that this wasn't about me personally but a murder trial in progress.

In earlier years, when I first started to explore meditation, I had been told by my teachers that the real art of spiritual inquiry is to sit in the fire of life, surrounded by flames of desire and passion, and become a silent, unmoving witness. In that courtroom, I had no choice. There was absolutely nothing else I could do but watch and witness.

Kelly Simmons, a Marin Superior Court Judge with ten years of experience behind her, was hearing the case. She was a serious-looking woman with delicate features, a perceptive manner, big glasses, and a narrow face framed with thick brown hair. When she entered the courtroom and sat down, taking in the scenario in front of her, a respectful silence descended on the room.

Immediately, Judge Simmons got down to the day's business, reading out the charges. The main ones were first-degree murder, lying in wait to kill, illegal possession of a handgun, and animal cruelty. Other charges included auto theft, possession of illegal drugs, and so on. I think there were 41 charges in all.

One by one, Judge Simmons asked the defendants how they pled to the charges, and all of them said, "Not guilty." The prosecution had anticipated this move, and Leon had already advised me it was a standard defense strategy during the preliminary stages of the court process, allowing time for negotiations.

For example, there was already talk among the prosecutors of making a plea bargain with Angold, offering him a reduced sentence if he agreed to testify against the other two.

Yet hearing these three killers plead "not guilty" in their own voices was sickening to me.

Not guilty? You have got to be kidding me.

For now, at least, the proceedings were over. Judge Simmons remanded the prisoners in custody pending trial and left the courtroom.

For a moment, I almost had to pinch myself to remember this was real and not a movie. I half expected a director's voice to yell, "Okay, cut! Take a break, everybody." The actors playing the prisoners would shed their chains, yawn and stretch, start chatting with those dressed as police officers, and drink coffee while waiting to film the next scene.

Of course, nothing like that happened. In the Hindu conception of the world as "maya," or illusion, we may all be actors in "Leela," a divine play of cosmic dimensions. But on the mundane level of day-to-day existence in Marin County, these three killers were facing an almost certain prospect of spending the rest of their lives in jail. They were led away. Wiebke and I said our farewells to Leon and Aicha and drove home.

I was proud of myself for having faced Steve's killers and that I had managed to remain calm, despite the intensity of the circumstances.

Much of the time, we don't give ourselves credit for what we have achieved. Instead, we shrug it off as if it was perfectly normal. To credit ourselves is often perceived as egotistical. And yet, in those extreme times, I had many opportunities to be generous with myself and practice self-appreciation and self-compassion, two essential ingredients to creating a positive life experience. I'm sure this attitude contributed to my healing.

Now I had to muster all my strength because the chemotherapy sessions weren't going well. During the most recent appointments, I couldn't even sit upright in the chemo chair. As I lay down with the drip in my arm, it felt like I was already in my coffin.

Wiebke sat next to the bed, and I'm certain it was difficult for her to see me like this, reminding her of the last days of our mother's life, when she was in the hospital, dying of breast cancer. I could see the sadness in her eyes. She wasn't crying. She was keeping herself together, but her pain was evident despite her best efforts to hide it.

Up until then I had endured four infusions of Adriamycin-Cytoxan, the so-called Red Devil, and another six of Taxol in combination with Carboplatin, the new course. This was my tenth chemo session, and it turned out to be my last for the time being. A routine check of my white blood cell count showed an alarming drop, while chemo side effects such as swollen hands and feet looked increasingly dramatic. My oncologist advised to wait with the next infusion until the cell count had improved.

Meanwhile, I asked Wiebke if she would drive me to Middletown and Harbin Hot Springs. The Valley Fire had scorched and ruined the area, and I had to go to the bank in Middletown. I wanted to see the devastation at Harbin for myself; I still couldn't quite believe that it was gone.

Middletown had been our local town. Steve and I would go to the post office, the bank, the grocery store, the Mexican restaurant for quesadillas, and meet people in the local café. It was an old-fashioned Californian town, not at all glamorous or touristy, that had grown out of being a stop for stagecoaches in the old days—offloading mail and passengers, changing the horses, and picking up supplies.

As we drove into town, I was stunned by what I saw: pure desolation. Trees were dead, buildings were gone, the remaining ones looked blackened, and even though the fires had long been extinguished, there was a heavy smell of smoke in the air. Pungent, pernicious fumes accompanied us wherever we went.

After completing some official paperwork at the bank, Wiebke and I drove along the road into the canyon where Harbin was located. Before the fire, this had been a gorgeous drive, lined with green meadows, oak and fir trees. It was a beautiful route leading to a beautiful place.

Now it was burned black, the earth scorched and bare. It was a wasteland. We didn't make it very far down the road because it was too painful for me to see the destruction.

Since then, the trees and grass have grown again, new buildings have been constructed, and the resort has reopened to the public. My friends encourage me to return there, to soak in the healing waters and embrace the New Harbin. Deep down, I know that going back would support me in confronting again that the old is dead and the new lives on. Yet I prefer my memories and cannot imagine ever revisiting Harbin.

Seven weeks after Steve's death, I conducted my own version of the "Phowa" ceremony for him, which, as I mentioned earlier, comes from the Tibetan Buddhist tradition. This practice is about envisioning a dead person's consciousness leaving the body and accepting the mystery of an individuality that persists after the body has died and been burned to ashes. The "Steveness" I had known and loved continues on its eternal journey, with my heartfelt good wishes for a beneficial and easy transition into the next form.

The ceremony is usually offered on each of the first seven days after a person dies and then again after 49 days to mark the end of the soul's transition from the body and the period of acute grieving. This was Day 49, and in performing the ritual I was able to find some solace.

Then came Thanksgiving, the first holiday since Steve died. In the past, we had spent most of our Thanksgiving dinners with Steve's family, who, true to tradition, would come together to celebrate the occasion. They had invited me to join them, but I was too fragile to travel and face the family without Steve. Instead,

Logan, Wiebke, and I lit celebratory candles and ate roast turkey with gravy, cranberry sauce, mashed potatoes, and pumpkin pie for dessert.

On the way to the airport the following afternoon, Wiebke and I gave ourselves time to make a detour to a beach on the Pacific coast of San Francisco. For late November, the weather was surprisingly warm and sunny. She was returning to face the bleak Danish winter, so to lie on our backs, chat, and watch the birds dance in the sky was a special treat. Despite the intensity of events, there were many moments, either with relatives, friends, or myself, when I could connect with the meditative, quiet internal part of me. This moment with Wiebke was one of them.

Before too long, my equanimity was replaced by a tidal wave of emotion. After seeing Wiebke off at the airport, I could hardly find my way back to my car because of the waterfall of unstoppable tears. When would I see her again? *Was* I ever going to see her again?

There was bad news about my treatment at the cancer care center. Several weeks earlier, when Steve had still been alive, a small growth had appeared on the scar from the surgery I had undergone in Costa Rica.

A biopsy had been performed on this lump. The result came back benign, and during the course of the Red Devil chemotherapy, it remained small and inactive. However, when the new chemo began, the growth started to get bigger. A week or so after the low white blood cell count, it was biopsied once more, and this time it was diagnosed as highly suspicious, a probable recurrence of cancer.

As predicted, the rare, triple negative metaplastic carcinoma was resistant to most chemotherapy forms. Only the Red Devil seemed to hold it back, but there was no possibility of continuing that treatment because four infusions were the maximum allowed dose. Any further dose would risk killing me.

Hence, it became clear that the Taxol-Carboplatin chemotherapy was ineffective. Dr. Susanna suggested an immediate PET Scan to let us know if, during the recent weeks of treatment, cancer had spread beyond my breast into the rest of my body.

It was pure torture waiting for the scan result. Sitting in the burning fire of not knowing, anxiously waiting for the phone to ring, flames of doubt and despair hungrily licking at me, challenged me to activate my entire repertoire of spiritual practice.

Eckart Tolle, a spiritual teacher and best-selling author whose work deeply resonates with me, has advised that when we catch ourselves waiting, we should try to connect with the present moment instead. Not so easy in my circumstances, but certainly possible.

What does it mean to be in the present moment? While waiting for the results, I could feel the air on my skin, notice my heart beating, listen to birds sing, and wonder at the mystery of life. This is available to us at any moment when we tune into the body and its senses. Our rational mind stops when we are connected to the body with full awareness. This is another one of the Tantric teachings that helped me through everything.

Even before this new development, I knew my chances of surviving were slim. Still, I was doing my best, cooperating with the treatment plan, visualizing a positive outcome, and giving my best to healing.

If it were now discovered that the cancer had spread into the lymph, bloodstream, and organs, it would bring an end to recovery and, indeed, to any future. Once again, I was teetering on a thin line between life and death.

When I lost my hair, I came to look upon this whole period as "the Great Dissolution." It started when Steve and I decided to move to Costa Rica, when everything that defined who I was in this world began to dissolve. First, we sold the house and almost all its contents, then we let go of the business, then we packed up our remaining belongings, said goodbye to our friends, and left the US.

Then I got cancer, and the dream of a happy retirement in Costa Rica disintegrated. We had to return to California for treatment. Then Harbin Hot Springs burned down, Steve was murdered, and cancer treatments destroyed whatever shred of health I still had.

In short, the image of "Lokita Carter" had completely disintegrated—who she was, what she did, how she looked, and how the world perceived her.

Only one fact remained: I was still alive. If the PET scan showed the cancer had metastasized, this last remaining thread would almost certainly be cut. I have never felt the sharp blade of the Grim Reaper's scythe pass closer to me than while waiting for that PET scan result.

CHAPTER 10

I AM NOT MY BREAST

"Lokita, can you imagine living with only one breast or not?"

Dr. Lynne Carrigan, the breast surgeon, was a tall, warm-hearted woman in her late thirties or early forties who had an excellent reputation as an advocate of women's health and a passionate commitment to saving as many lives as possible.

The PET scan revealed that the rest of my body was cancer free, so now we could move forward.

After Dr. Lynne had examined my breasts, we sat down and talked about surgery. "Let me tell you what your options are. The cancer you have, Lokita, doesn't usually return in the other breast. It's a strange cancer, behaving in a completely random way. It's almost not like a breast cancer at all, but it just so happens to be in the breast." This made me think about Dr. Heraldo and his "bad luck" comment.

For this reason, Dr. Lynne said she wouldn't recommend a double mastectomy since the other breast was healthy and unlikely to be affected.

"Have you thought about reconstruction?"

"Honestly, I'm not sure what to think. I have mixed feelings about it."

Dr. Lynne explained that reconstruction could be done with an implant or by taking some fatty tissue from another part of the body.

Since I was all skin and bones and there wasn't a shred of fatty tissue anywhere on my body, and I didn't want to get an implant, I decided I wouldn't have reconstruction. With that, Dr. Lynne scheduled the surgery for December 15th.

Somewhere I had seen a painting of twelve women of all shapes, colors, and sizes with either one breast or none at all. This confronting image had brought tears to my eyes, yet it also gave me hope and reassurance that I would still be beautiful after the mastectomy.

"You have breast cancer and will get a mastectomy" does not mean the same as, "You will no longer be an attractive woman." What exactly defines our beauty?

I was born severely cross-eyed and had to undergo several corrective eye surgeries before the age of six. For many years I wore glasses, with one eye covered with a black patch. I was often told that I was ugly. In a photo of me as a young girl, I am smiling wholeheartedly into the camera, with my eyes turning inward toward my nose. Even nowadays, I still feel the stab in my heart when people laugh at the photo. I grew up feeling ugly. Yet as I became a teenager, for some reason, I was attractive to people, especially men. My friends often commented that it was a miracle I could get any man I wanted, given how I looked. I came to realize that what was perceived as exterior ugliness was outweighed by who I was, my qualities, my humor, and a unique inner light that shone through my eyes. Beauty became a quality rather than a set of features. By the way, my eyes finally became normal in my thirties after a final operation.

Some five years after the mastectomy, I enjoyed a brief love affair. He was a kind and skillful lover, and when he stroked my breastless left side, I had the distinct sensation that there was still a breast with a nipple. Maybe it was like one of those phantom experiences after an amputation. After our lovemaking, I told him about it, and he said, "Well, it did feel like there was still a breast there."

While awaiting the mastectomy, I wrote a letter to my breast and thanked her for having been my lovely companion. After all, we had been together since puberty.

I thanked her for being shapely and sexy and for protecting me by not spreading cancer to other parts of my body. I thanked her for all the good moments we had together, with Steve and other lovers before him. At the end, I said goodbye to her.

On the day of my surgery, I was accompanied to the hospital by Mary Alice, who had been providing so much unwavering support, and Tracy, who had come from Mexico to be there for the operation and stay with me for a couple of weeks afterwards.

Even though I was going to be at the hospital for only one night, I brought along my special quilt and favorite soft toy: a furry, white Tibetan snow leopard I'd bought in Australia many years earlier. I wanted to wake up after the operation in my comfort zone rather than an anonymous hospital bed.

A nurse escorted us to a pre-op room.

"We would like to wait right here with Lokita." Mary Alice was insistent. The nurse nodded.

"Yes, and we'd like to be with her, if possible, until she gets wheeled through the door of the operating theater." Tracy was very clear. The nurse nodded again.

Dr. Lynne entered the room with a thick purple marker pen and swiftly drew all over my breast and chest. "We're going to cut here, and we're going to cut there, and we're going to do this and that…."

Tracy and Mary Alice took photos and showed them to me. I saw myself in the surgical gown with purple marks all over the breast about to be amputated. It was both confronting, sad, and at the same time, bizarrely funny.

Dr. Lynne was matter of fact, loving, and kind. We laughed together at the drawings she made on my skin. Even in this, the most desperate of times, I somehow found humor.

"May I make a request?"

She nodded.

"In TV medical dramas, I've seen scenes taking place in the operating theater during surgery, and there was small talk going on between the doctors and nurses. Does that happen during operations? Because I'd rather it didn't during mine."

I recalled images of medical teams—admittedly actors in soap operas—chatting about their personal problems while performing life-threatening surgery.

Dr. Lynne understood my concern. "Most of the time, we only talk about what we're doing with the patient. So, if you don't want us to speak about anything other than the practical medical stuff, that will be fine. I can also ask my team to pray for a favorable outcome of your surgery."

That felt good. "One more thing. If you were to play any background music, it would be lovely to have calm and peaceful music, perhaps with nature sounds."

Somehow, I didn't like the idea of disco music, hip-hop, or reggae being played while I was under the knife.

Dr. Lynne agreed. "Yes, sure, we have the right thing for you." With her white medical coat flapping like wings, she dashed off into the operating theater to get ready.

I lay down on a surgical bed, which would be rolled into the theater for the operation. It was cold and uncomfortable at first, but the plastic top sheet with which I was covered turned out to be inflatable, transforming into a floating blanket. The surprise of it rising when filled with warm air made me giggle. By then, they had probably given me some "happy juice," a pre-op injection to keep me relaxed, which no doubt contributed to my amusement.

In the operating theatre, I was met by Dr. Lynne with her operating gear on—mask, hair net, outfit, and everything—and a whole team of nurses and an anesthesiologist. Before going under, I looked around and felt I was in safe, caring hands.

When I woke up, I was in a hospital bed with my favorite quilt, my cuddly snow leopard in the crook of my arm. Tracy and Mary Alice were sitting next to my bed, looking at me with radiant smiles. They were full of sweet praises.

There was a soft knock on the door, and Dr. Lynne appeared. "I'd like to be the first to tell you the good news."

She explained that she had removed the cancer with big margins, and there was no sign of it in my ribcage and nothing in a biopsy of the lymph nodes. In short, there was no sign of cancer anywhere, and now it was time to let the wound heal. I had officially reached an important milestone: NED—no evidence of disease. In cancer language, we also speak of this as "dancing with Ned."

We gently hugged, and I thanked her for telling me so soon after the operation. Waiting for pathology reports on top of the mastectomy would have been agonizing.

As planned, I stayed one night in the hospital, and the next morning, Tracy wheeled me out in a wheelchair and took me home, where she fed me mountains of comfort food in the form of fresh, homemade waffles. Waffles had never tasted as good as on that morning!

The next few days were a blur of feelings, ranging from deep grief and despair for everything I had lost—my husband, my health, my breast—to a sense of relief and gratitude that the cancer was finally gone.

My upper rib cage was under a thick, all-around bandage, with a couple of thin tubes ending in reservoirs to allow liquid from the wound to drain. It was my task to empty these several times a day, and I did this diligently because I knew that this routine was a step on the path to healing.

I went to see Dr. Lynne for my follow-up appointment a week later. By that time, the wound had dried, and when she removed the bandage, it didn't look as radical as I had feared. I had seen photos of long, unsightly mastectomy scars, with lumpy ridges of flesh where the breast had been, but mine was nothing like that.

Mine appeared smooth and flat, like a boy's chest without a nipple. There was no excess tissue. The scar line itself looked neat and clean, and I imagined that it would fade and virtually disappear with time.

When I look at my reflection in the mirror these days, I see the image of the Hindu deity Ardhanarishvara. One side of the body is male, the other female, representing the union of man and woman within, merging external and internal qualities to form perfect harmony and timeless beauty. Knowing that my body showed this Tantric symbolism helped me accept my one-breasted reality and not feel inadequate as a woman.

In this way, it was a continuation of the process that had started earlier on my cancer journey when I had begun chemotherapy. I knew my hair would fall out, so I cut it short, then shaved my head completely.

Back then, I said, "I'm not my hair," and although I had enjoyed it with all its shininess and length, I understood that I couldn't define myself through my appearance. Whether I had hair was irrelevant because this person, Lokita, was still the same person.

Seeing my chest after the mastectomy, I realized, "Oh, I'm not my breast either!"

And was I still here? Was I, Lokita, still fully present? Yes. I was still the one, whether I had one or two breasts or maybe none at all. So, who was this "I"? What was this mysterious "Lokitaness"?

I decided to create an affirmation for myself: "I'm a luminous being, strong and beautiful, going through a very intense phase of my life."

The more I said that to myself, the more I could embody it. Even when thoughts of pain came or I was tossed around by waves of grief, I could remind myself. It helped me stay in touch with that truth.

A similar, extremely powerful realization was transmitted to me during a session with my therapist, Dr. Matt.

It happened during one of several occasions when I was so desperate and bereaved that I wanted to die. I couldn't see beyond the present moment into a future. I said to Dr. Matt, "Look, I'm sorry. I can't do this anymore. I can't do this living anymore. I'm going to have to check out of this life. I don't have the courage. I don't have the power. I don't have the strength. I just want to be dead."

I shall never forget what he said to me. It was one of the most significant and profound statements I had ever heard. Dr. Matt looked at me with great compassion and sincerity, saying, "Lokita, I have to tell you something." He paused for a moment. "You are already dead."

It was like seeing the light. It was true. All exterior definitions of what I had formerly thought of as Lokita, or as part of Lokita, were gone: my house, my business, my past at Harbin Hot Springs, my health, my husband, my hair, my breast. All those aspects that had helped to shape my identity were dead.

There was only this pure mystery called Lokita. The undeniable truth was that I was alive, as a pure presence, as pure consciousness stripped of all its clothing. Naked, alone, shining from some unnamable source, I continued to be.

This extraordinary moment with Dr. Matt gave me a new level of acceptance of how things were, an understanding that even when everything is taken away, this mysterious being is still here.

Following the success of the surgery, there was more good news coming my way. Coco was being returned to me. Cindy from the Marin Humane Society delivered her to my house just before Christmas.

Coco had been ready since the end of November, but we all felt it would be better if she came home after my mastectomy so I could have some extra days of recovery by myself.

Coco was ecstatic to see me, running around the house, checking out everything, her ears curled up in a way that, for her, indicated great joy. She sneezed with happiness and excitement.

The left side of her face was still swollen from the series of operations to her jaw, but she was healing well, and there was nothing more to be done at UC Davis.

They say a dog mirrors the qualities of the human who owns it, and sometimes they say a dog even looks like the human they are with. Well, obviously, Coco didn't exactly look like Steve or me, but with her return, it felt at least some part of our family was together again, which was lovely and healing for my heart.

That first night, we slept 14 hours straight. I was exhausted, and it seemed Coco was, too. So we crashed in bed. It was as if I had a big, soft, life-sized, breathing toy lying next to me.

When I woke up in the morning, I felt better than I had in a long time.

Soon, the question arose, "Should I take Coco to the trail where Steve was killed? Could it retraumatize the dog as much as it could retraumatize a human being?"

I decided to take the risk and drove us both to Gunshot Fire Road. The sun was bright on this cool and clear December morning. It was quiet and peaceful, and I occasionally heard a crow squawking in the distance. Coco was delighted to be off leash. This was probably her first unrestrained run since she had been shot. She skipped along happily, enjoying the freedom, sniffing around in the bushes, checking out which other dogs had passed by—"reading the newspaper," as they call it—because a dog's nose tells them all the recent news.

The spot where Steve had died was no longer just scrappy grass, dirt, and bloodstains. Instead, it had become an altar of love, grief, and healing.

Friends from our tantric community had held a ceremony there and left a stone with the inscription, "How much more can you love? – Steve Carter." For many, it resonated as Steve's ultimate reminder. It was the question he had often asked in workshops when things became difficult and hurdles seemed insurmountable.

A generous artist had donated a memorial plaque made of steel, imprinted with a photo of Steve and inscribed with some explanatory text. The area of the altar was by now ten square feet in size, or bigger, and full of flowers.

As we approached, I watched Coco closely. In the weeks since the killing, it had rained, and the stains were no longer visible, but I imagined that Coco's sensitive nose could still smell the blood that had flowed here not so long ago.

At the altar, Coco stopped for a few moments, then wandered around, smelling the pictures, the flowers, and other items.

And then?

She ran off, heading down the trail, doing her doggy thing, poking her nose into holes in the ground, and once in a while, looking back at me as if to say, "Hey, Lokita, are you coming or what?"

What went on in Coco's mind, I'll never know. She simply ran ahead of me into her life, full of joy and curiosity about nature waiting to be explored.

Seeing Coco so alive and happy, so present and "in the moment," cracked me wide open. I cried tears of happiness and sadness together. Locked into tragedy, I hadn't walked on the trail past the spot where Steve died; nothing beyond it had existed for me. As I meandered onwards, I could see a blurred vision of life free from pain and suffering.

It gave me the strength and courage to move forward and begin focusing positively on my future, if only for this moment, because there were more hurdles ahead for me to clear.

As I watched Coco's simple enjoyment, a soft, light breeze of hope brushed against my tear-stained cheeks. With Coco came the much-needed reminder that it's possible to rekindle a sense of happiness and lightness of heart even under the most tragic circumstances.

Yes, Coco was fine. It was me who needed to regain my love and enthusiasm for life.

CHAPTER 11

TREATMENT & TESTIMONY

Shortly after New Year's Day, 2016, almost three months after Steve's murder, I received a call from an official in the Marin County planning department who asked me to remove the sacred objects, flowers, and photos from the spot on Gunshot Fire Road where Steve had been shot dead.

"With due respect, it's public land," he explained. "It's not permitted. Can you please take it away?"

"Yes, of course, I'll remove it," I agreed. "But, in its place, I'd like to install a plaque to memorialize what happened there so that people can be reminded that an innocent man was shot dead at this spot on a public trail. Would that be possible?"

"You'd need to file an application. If everything was in order, we could have a meeting and discuss it."

"Oh, good. Thanks for your help. I'll take care of it tomorrow."

The next morning, I went to the trail to figure out how I would remove the items. Almost everything was gone.

The only thing left was the memorial plaque I wanted Marin County to approve, ideally set into a stone column.

The area had been raked clean. It looked neat and tidy as if nothing had ever happened there. It was just an ordinary trail, with ordinary trees and shrubs, ordinary dirt, and ordinary grass.

I called the county office, but nobody seemed to know about it. I called the park rangers, the police, and everyone I could think of, but I drew a blank. Nobody was taking responsibility.

At the *Marin Independent Journal*, I talked to one of their reporters.

"I'd already agreed to take it away," I explained. "I would have gone there with some friends. We would have created a little ceremony and cleared the space. But they didn't give us a chance."

I even spoke to a reporter on local radio, appealing to the person who had taken the things away to at least have the decency to drop them off at some location, then make an anonymous call to the radio station to say where they had been left so that I could pick them up. But there was no response.

It was an ugly situation. Who would do such a thing? Somebody, a real person, was responsible. But nobody would admit to having taken away the tributes for a murdered man before his widow had a chance to do so herself, with dignity and grace. I was furious and heartbroken at the same time.

However, the hot pain mixed with the burning anger had an unexpected side effect. I felt more empowered than I had for ages, ready for just about anything. My inner life force was reawakening.

In fairness to the county supervisors, I must mention that Marin County officials approved the application to change the trail's name some months later. Spearheaded by friends and supported by the local community, it was felt that Gunshot Fire Road was simply too evocative and a painful reminder of what happened there. The name was changed to Sunrise Fire Road, a heartwarming symbol of resurrection and rebirth.

Often, during those long weeks of chemotherapy and mourning for Steve, in my bleakest moments, I had asked myself, "What is the meaning of life? What is life's purpose? Why am I still alive?" Now I realize that when life force is restored, it itself provides the answer, not as a concept, not as a philosophy, but as a powerful and intrinsic sense of knowing. I'm alive simply to be alive. That's life's purpose—nothing more and nothing less.

My medical team was expecting me to start radiation as the next step. However, since I was haunted by the possibility that there might still be stray cancer cells roaming around in my body which had gone unnoticed by the PET scan, I felt drawn to a course of adjuvant chemotherapy, which takes place after a cancerous tumor has been removed. I learned about this regimen from a Facebook group of women with the same cancer. Developed by a doctor in Texas, it had shown promising results. Although nasty side effects were reported by many in the group, I was determined to "throw the kitchen sink" at the cancer to ensure none of it was left in my body.

My oncologist was hesitant because the information came from a Facebook group. However, remembering that I needed to be my own best advocate, I was adamant. Finally, Dr. Susanna spoke with the doctor in Texas and other specialist oncologists before agreeing to go ahead with the treatment.

Even though I was my own cheerleader rooting for another round of chemo, returning to treatment was scary. What side effects was I going to have this time? Fatigue? Nausea? Or would it be the dreaded hand-foot syndrome again? Or perhaps hair loss, just when I was beginning to feel good about my newly hairy legs as they recovered from previous rounds.

For me, chemo was always a radical journey into the unknown, mirroring the underlying truth of life itself. We never really know what will happen next.

Much later, in an interview, I was asked whether, due to the unbelievably tragic circumstances, I felt abandoned by God.

I answered, "No, not at all. The divine mystery is everywhere, in every moment. The only way I can ever feel abandoned by God is if I abandon myself, my essence, my deep core of stillness and knowing—and for me, this is impossible."

I wasn't always as certain as I sounded in that interview, but it did reflect the underlying foundation of my trust in life that has always been with me.

The new chemotherapy program began on January 15th, 2016. The infusion appointments went pretty much the same way as before, combined with a daily oral dose of an immunotherapy drug, but the side effects were gruesome. Soon, I developed open sores inside my mouth, in the lining and the gums, much larger than the common type of mouth sores. Some of them were the size of a quarter.

My entire mouth was afflicted with them. It was excruciatingly painful. For seven weeks, I struggled to eat and sleep, and I could barely speak. One friend made me blended soups, others brought me protein drinks, while another gave me a thick glass straw that I could position at the back of my mouth to avoid the sores while sucking on it. This is how I "ate" for seven weeks—through a thick glass straw.

I tried various mouthwashes to reduce the pain, but nothing worked. Finally, one sympathetic and creative pharmacist took pity on me and developed a lidocaine-loaded concoction that, when swished around the mouth, would lay a temporary film over the wounds so that I could suck on the straw with less pain.

By the end, however, I had to resort to using oral morphine to get some relief and sleep. Even then, I had to lie with my mouth wide open so the sores wouldn't touch my tongue or teeth.

After six weeks and two infusions, I yielded to Dr. Susanna's suggestion to discontinue the treatment. Whatever benefits I might be receiving were more than outweighed by the side effects.

My final chemo session was on February 26th. It was the same day my mother had died from breast cancer nine years earlier. I was still embracing life at a time when death could well have sent me after her.

This, my third and last chemotherapy regimen, was an extremely hard process, but it left me with a feeling of achievement of having done everything I could. I felt then and still do today that this last chemotherapy drug cocktail contributed to the demise of the cancer.

My treatment journey was almost over. The only remaining part was radiation. After a couple of weeks of recovery time, I met the radiation oncologist, Dr. Melanie Harrison. She was a highly respected authority in her field and exuded warmth, compassion, and a sense of refinement. I took to her immediately and appreciated her honesty and insightfulness.

A few days into the radiation sessions, she recommended Joan Didion's best-selling memoir, *The Year of Magical Thinking*, which tells the story of how the author went through the first year after losing her husband, out of the blue, to a heart attack on Christmas Day.

When Dr. Melanie told me about the book, it was with great hesitation. Given that I was acutely grieving for Steve, she wasn't sure the book would be good for my psychological makeup. Maybe it would throw me into a deep depression and loneliness. However, I started reading it that night and felt quite the opposite: I wasn't alone in my loss and sadness.

The course of radiation was set for 25 sessions, given daily during weekdays, with a break at the weekend so that the entire treatment would last five weeks. Its purpose was to eradicate any stray cancer cells lurking in the rib cage or the area where my breast had been.

A few days before the first radiation session, I had to come in for preparation. I was asked to lie down on the sliding stretcher of the radiation machine with my left arm above my head while a custom foam form was created to hold my body in a certain position to ensure that the same area received radiation every time.

One weirdly entertaining aspect was how the radiation technicians referred to the area that needed to be treated. I had already grown accustomed to the idea that, once my breast had gone, the remaining flat area was deemed a "chest." But now it was referred to as "the field," with other defining terms such as "superclav" and "medial bolus tangent."

In addition, each area was filled with a bewildering assortment of numbers. In their communication during the treatment, the technicians asked each other questions like, "Okay, let's call back Lokita's settings. Did you do the setup for 7 to 53? Yes, right, and after that, are we doing 1:10, okay, now at 53:7?"

A large area of my chest, designated by four small tattoo marks, formed the basic "field," in the shape of a square, extending from the center of my collarbone to my left shoulder, then down my left side to the lower rib cage, across to the sternum in the middle, and up to the center of the collarbone once more. My right nipple became an "anatomical landmark."

Throughout each session, I had to remain completely motionless for 20 to 40 minutes—no coughing, twitching, or moving a muscle. If I had wanted to scratch an itch anywhere on my body, I would have had to ask for it to be done by someone else.

To stay calm and relaxed, I put on my sleep mask and recited soundlessly the 12-syllable mantra of Padmasambhava, the Indian mystic who brought Buddhism to Tibet in the eighth century. Steve and I had taught it countless times in our workshops to call forth his transformative powers, blessings, and healing energies.

Om ah hum vajra guru padma siddhi hum. Om ah hum vajra guru padma siddhi hum. Om ah hum vajra guru padma siddhi hum.

To receive radiation for 25 days sounded easy enough, but my assumption that it would be without side effects was mistaken. Although the actual radiation couldn't be seen nor felt, whatever was emitted by the machine burned the skin, and it got progressively worse as the treatment advanced. The skin became pink, then red, then brown, and finally started to peel away.

To prevent serious damage, I had to coat the area with a special, thick, greasy ointment, then cover it with a cotton T-shirt to avoid spoiling my outer clothes.

After each session and several times during the day, I did this with a positive attitude, saying to myself, "I'm lovingly spreading this ointment on my beautiful upper body, my chest, and my heart chakra, with kind and gentle strokes, appreciating my skin and its warmth and perfection…."

Whether it was because of the ointment, my positive affirmations, or both, the radiation burns on my chest didn't become oozing wounds, which was the case with some women.

Close to the end of the five weeks, the continuous radiation was taking such a toll on my energy that I dragged myself to the cancer care center each day, shuffling around slowly rather than walking. Friends drove me to the sessions, and afterwards, I would lie down on my bed like a zombie with Coco by my side. My chest looked burnt and crispy brown, and I was exhausted.

And suddenly, after eight long months, the cancer treatment was over. No more chemo, no more radiation, no more blood tests. And I was still alive. I had imagined that the last day of treatment would be a celebration. Instead, I wished Steve was there to share the moment with me. He would have been so proud of me.

Throughout this ordeal, I discovered that time is elastic. The eight months from August to April passed like a blink of an eye. At the same time, they were the longest months of my life. The minutes and hours had seemed endless. Yet they had gone by in an instant. It made me wonder how it would be when I died. Would the long, eventful years of my life melt into one short moment?

Through the cancer care center, I signed up to participate in "Horses as Healers," a therapeutic program for those who had completed cancer treatment. It was held at a large horse ranch in the Western part of Marin. My sister had been into horses all her life, but I had been bitten in the back by one when I was 11, so horses didn't do much for me. However, I was willing to give it a try.

The rural environment of the ranch in the spring, with its abundant California poppies and wide green fields, inspired health and recovery. I was assigned a small Norwegian Fjord horse specially trained for therapy. In stature, she was more like a sturdy little pony, adorable with her caramel coat of hair and a blond forelock that fell across her face. In the three sessions I attended, I learned basic steps of horsemanship, slowly riding her in large circles around a covered hall, then taking her back out to her field after brushing her hair and feeding her treats.

These sessions proved helpful. I enjoyed this cowgirl experience: wearing my red checkered fleece-lined shirt, tight jeans, and sturdy

Australian Redback booties, taking in the smell of the horses, stables, and nature. Feelings of peacefulness, even optimism, surged through me like new lifeblood. I could do this. Despite everything that had happened, I could do normal things that were fun and uplifting.

With the end of the treatment, I was officially a cancer survivor. Normally, this would be a reason for celebration. Yet given the high rate of recurrence of this type of cancer, a permanent shadow hung over me, the shadow of a possible return of the disease, its progression, and my eventual death.

In reality, everyone has to face the same circumstance. We are all living on borrowed time, and we will all arrive at the same destination. But it's different to know it intellectually than have it thrust in one's face. My time had suddenly become more precious, and I began to choose my activities as wisely as possible, since it could all end at any moment, and I would find myself sitting in that chemo chair all over again, or worse.

The adage, "Live every day as if it was your last and also as if it was the first day of your life," took on new meaning. What would I do differently if this was the last or first day? I wanted to live this way, intensely and vitally.

My next priority was to leave the United States and put physical distance between me and the events of the past months. Having to deal with cancer had been challenging enough and would have been hard on anybody. But my husband being murdered at the same time was so devastating that my intrinsic "fight or flight" response kicked into high gear.

While I couldn't fight cancer or Steve's death, the flight response propelled my yearning to run fast and get away from it all. I needed to be in Germany, my original homeland, with my family and old friends, speaking my native language. I needed to recover in my happy place, the island of Sylt in the far North.

It made no sense to leave California until now because it had been necessary to complete the cancer treatment. I was also determined to attend the court proceedings as much as possible. Strangely, seeing those responsible for Steve's death and knowing they would be held accountable for their actions gave me strength. I wanted to do it for Steve, too, since he wasn't there to do it for himself. I couldn't avenge his death, but at least I could sit there, his widow, a visible reminder for the killers to see what they had done.

The US at large had morphed into a representation of the violence, murder, loss, and grief I had experienced. I was counting the days until I could depart, at least for the foreseeable future.

There was a sweet tradition in our family, started by my mother when my sister and I were children, to track the days leading up to our annual summer vacations camping on our favorite island Sylt.

One hundred days before we were due to leave, my mother would hang up a tape measure, the kind used for sewing or knitting, of one hundred centimeters in length, and every day my sister and I were allowed to cut off one centimeter. In this way, we could excitedly watch our vacation coming closer and closer.

I did the same for my exit from the US. To give myself enough time to recover from the radiation treatment and allow room for any delays or unexpected events, I decided to leave three weeks after the radiation treatment was completed. Exactly one hundred days before departure, I hung up my tape—in inches rather than centimeters—and cut off one inch for every day that passed.

Around this time, I received notice that our VW Jetta, which had been held as evidence in the homicide case, could now be returned to me. Even merely *seeing* that car again was the last thing I wanted, never mind driving it! Ultimately, it was returned to George, the car salesman, who eventually resold it and sent me a check with the proceeds.

Sometimes I imagine who might now be driving around in that car. Did they know whose car it was before they bought it? Everything has its own story, and the car wasn't an exception. Nowadays, I still feel a punch in the stomach when I pass a silver Jetta station wagon.

Then Leon and Aicha, the prosecuting attorneys in Steve's murder trial, told me I would be required to appear in person as a witness at the preliminary hearing later that year.

My flight was booked, and I informed them of my decision. "On April 20th," I said, "my treatment will be finished, and I'm going to stay in the United States until May 11th. After that, I leave. The latest date I can give the court is May 9th."

They understood and talked to the judge. A special court session was arranged to accommodate my departure plans. I invited my closest friends to attend the hearing. Afterwards, there was to be a farewell luncheon.

On the day I was due to give evidence, I was nervous. This time, I wasn't going to sit in the audience. This time I would be asked to take the witness stand, and people would be looking at me while the courtroom artist would probably be drawing my picture for the media.

I would be on public display for the first time in the court proceedings. I was shaky but also driven by the prospect that I would leave California in two days. Then it would be over.

After arriving at the Marin Civic Center, I was ushered into an anteroom before being called into the courtroom. Again, I found myself in a movie-like scene with familiar lines like, "Will the witness please take the stand?" I had to vow to tell the truth; then I was allowed to sit.

The defendants sat across from me. At this stage in the proceedings, they were still called "defendants" because they weren't convicted yet, but they had killed Steve and Audrey, and everyone in the courtroom knew it. They didn't look at me, keeping their heads down.

The shooter, Lampley, was closest to me, then Alligood, who had been Lampley's girlfriend, then Angold.

Behind them sat my friends, and behind them again was the row of police officers, strapping, handsome, alert-looking men, and stern, strong-looking women in their uniforms, emanating a sense of safety and security.

Leon, for the prosecution, asked me a series of questions. "What is your name? What was your relationship to Steve Carter? Where were you at the time of the murder? At whose house were you staying? What were you doing?" And so on.

My heart was pounding. My hands were moist with sweat. The wooden bench on the witness stand was hard. I looked at the sea of faces, my throat tight and my breath short. That morning I had put on a scarf to disguise the red blotches that usually bloom on my neck when things get stressful. I arranged the fabric now to hide how nervous I was feeling.

My loud voice cut the air across the courtroom when I answered the questions. Every single word came out of my mouth like a sharp dagger. I would have liked to say so many things to the murderers of my beloved, but I needed to follow the court procedure.

There were questions like, "What time did Mr. Carter leave the house? What was he wearing? When was he coming back? What was written in the text message you received from him? At what time did you receive it?"

At some point, the female suspect, Lila Alligood, raised her head and looked directly at me as I spoke. She was crying. "At least one of them shows some human emotion," I thought. I could feel that my love for Steve and the pain of losing him had touched her heart.

"Thank you, Mrs. Carter. We have everything we need," concluded Leon.

The defense attorneys asked me a couple of questions, including, "In which pocket did Mr. Carter usually keep his wallet?"

I closed my eyes and saw Steve in front of me, wearing his favorite cargo pants with the many pockets. He smiled, and I watched as he reached into his top right pocket to pull out his wallet. This was important because one of the bullets had been fired into Steve's hip, passing through his wallet and staining the notes with blood.

"The right top pocket."

The questions came to an end. Since this hearing was only held to take my witness statement, the judge thanked me, a police inspector escorted me out of the courtroom, and the session was closed.

My friends and I met in the parking lot and drove home to Terra Linda where a delicious lunch was waiting for us.

I was still physically weak and emotionally exhausted and, therefore, not a particularly active hostess. But I was smiling and laughing, mostly with relief, because everything had been completed. Finally, I could leave.

CHAPTER 12

THE GREAT ESCAPE

"Oh my gosh, Lokita, it's so good to see you! I can't believe what you've been through since we last saw each other! You must be beyond exhausted!"

With tears in his eyes, my Danish friend Bjarke threw his arms around me and enveloped me in a big, comforting hug at the check-in counter at the San Francisco airport. "It's all over now, darling. You're safe now. It's all over."

Bjarke worked as a flight attendant for Scandinavian Airlines. We had been able to coordinate our schedules so that we were on the same flight—me as a passenger, he as part of the crew.

Then, looking over my shoulder, he noticed the five suitcases and Coco's large travel kennel. "Looks like you're planning to stay for a while!" We both laughed.

"Yes, I sure am!" Adrenaline flushed through me. "And I'm so touched that you are here. Thank you. It feels like I'm finally able to come home."

As my plane began to pull away from the gangway, nestled comfortably in my seat, I took a sip of the champagne Bjarke had brought me. The bubbles exploded like liquid confetti in my mouth, intensifying my elation.

At last I was on the way to Copenhagen. After spending a few days at Bjarke's home, I would travel to Wiebke and her family in Southern Denmark and from there across the border to Northern Germany, where I planned to spend several weeks resting and recuperating on my favorite island Sylt. Copenhagen was my first stop on the journey back home. Not only back home to my roots and family but, I suspected, also back home to myself.

The liftoff from the runway was glorious. The Bay Area, with the Golden Gate Bridge bathed in the last light of the setting sun, disappeared beneath me, leaving the whole nightmare behind. Within minutes I fell into a deep sleep and melted into the seat, disappearing into the neutral, timeless zone of flying away.

Bjarke met me again after deboarding and helped reunite me with Coco at customs. The sliding glass doors opened, and I stepped outside the airport building into the cool Danish air. That first full breath refreshed my entire being.

Bjarke and Lars, a married couple for some 12 years whom I had befriended a few years earlier after our chance meeting in Costa Rica, welcomed us into their home, a charming white house set in a manicured garden, with rooms spread over three floors. The boys schlepped the luggage to my room, their exuberant dog welcomed Coco, and their cat dashed at high speed into the bushes. Thus began a most relaxing and healing week with my friends.

The interior of their house was warm and tasteful, decorated in an understated Nordic way. The books on their shelves were sorted by color so that a rainbow of volumes lined their living room wall. A big comfortable sofa became our nest for the next few days. The three of us would lie back on the cozy couch, snuggled under our blankets, watching movies, laughing, talking, hanging out, eating, having cups of tea, and snoozing off, all the while accompanied by our pets.

Above all, the drama that had happened was far away in some distant land, and I could relax and enjoy the love and closeness I had missed so much since Steve died. Simple moments like these opened my heart and flushed away the pain and grief, lightening my step. I remembered that a "normal" life existed in which radical events such as chemotherapy-resistant breast cancer and random shootings were not the norm but distant, blurred images on the outskirts of daily reality.

A difficult aspect of having cancer and dealing with Steve's murder was knowing that nothing would ever be the same again. There was no respite from this reality. Every morning it would be there waiting for me when I opened my eyes. Facing the unfaceable, even accepting it, living with it, and somehow moving forward took a lot of courage.

Everyone who has lost a loved one, been life-threateningly ill, or had to deal with trauma will relate to this. Will there ever be lightness and joy again?

After the time with Bjarke and Lars, I was reunited with Wiebke and Gerhard, their children, and my father. Because I hadn't been sure I would be able to see them again, it was especially precious to spend a week together.

And at last, the moment for quiet time alone arrived, and I could finally attempt to come to terms with and begin to integrate what had happened in the past year.

For my self-prescribed retreat, I rented a vacation home on the island of Sylt, Germany's most northerly point. With its long white beaches, cool fresh sea air, wandering sand dunes, and abundant *Wadden Sea* nature, Sylt was where I felt most at home.

I dedicated six glorious weeks of time out without dealing with anybody, explaining anything, or fulfilling any obligations or expectations. At last, I was anonymous. Nobody recognized me as "the cancer-stricken widow of the man murdered by the three drifters in Fairfax," which, because of the ongoing news coverage, was happening regularly in Marin County.

But even here, so far from California, the past didn't leave me entirely. Outwardly, Coco's face was the cause. We would walk on the beach, along the edge of the wild North Sea, breathing in the salty air, sand between our toes, and our noses freezing in the fierce wind. A passer-by would turn their head. "Oh, what a lovely dog! Is it a Doberman?"

"Yes. She is the greatest dog! Her name is Coco!" I would instantly turn into a proud mom.

When they came closer, they noticed Coco had only one eye and inevitably would ask, "But why does she have only one eye?"

In the beginning, I would tell the truth on a couple of occasions. "She got shot in the eye."

This, naturally, triggered the next question, "Goodness gracious! How did that happen to the poor dog?"

Then the whole story would come flooding out of me, accompanied by tears and grief. The passer-by would shake their head in disbelief.

"Where did this happen? What a shocking story!" Then they would cover their eyes with their hands, look at their watch discreetly, and suddenly be in a hurry to leave. "Well, all the best to you!" And with that, they were gone.

After a while, I decided not to tell the story anymore. It was too much. People were expecting a pleasant conversation and didn't want to know that my husband was shot dead on a trail in California just when I was undergoing chemotherapy treatment. Nor did I wish to keep repeating the tale.

So, I changed the narrative. "She had an accident," I'd say.

That didn't work so well either because the next question would invariably be, "Oh, I'm sorry to hear that. Poor dog! What kind of accident?" If there were children present, they would be extra curious and ask, "Was it a bicycle accident, or was it a car accident?"

I thought, "Okay, I can't say that anymore either!"

Finally, I came up with the perfect answer. When people inquired, "What happened?" I replied, "My dog was born this way."

Almost everyone would accept my explanation. "That's amazing. She looks like a happy dog."

"Yes, she sure is." That said, our conversation would veer off in other directions, such as the weather, the food in the restaurants, the beauty of the island, and so on. From then on, this little white lie became my smooth way out of an awkward situation.

The six weeks on Sylt were quiet, introspective, and deeply healing. Often Coco and I just sat by the sea, watching the waves, listening to the screeching of the seagulls overhead as if it was a nightingale's melodious song. To me, it was. It was the sound of home.

Fortunately, I was beginning to eat again and indulged myself with my favorite North German Island foods: *Bratkartoffeln und Brathering*, fried potatoes with herring, and *Krabbenbrötchen*, bread roll sandwiches with shrimp. Participating in gentle aquatic exercise classes in a heated pool several times a week rounded off my wellness program.

After my retreat on Sylt, I rented a small house close to my sister's home and made myself comfortable there. It was in the middle of nowhere and had a large garden perfect for Coco to run around, chasing rabbits and mice.

However, I noticed that Coco was still traumatized from all she had been through and wasn't listening to me as well as in the past, so I consulted with Monika, a dog psychologist and trainer who also offered boarding services for canines.

Monika was a vibrant woman with a mane of blonde hair, an exuberant manner, a positive outlook on life, and, of course, a great passion for dogs. On her large ranch, she had all kinds of fun activities set up for her canine guests. There were see-saws, agility tunnels to run through, hurdles to jump over, colorful cones for a dog slalom, large balls, and many other challenges and entertainment.

It was our first meeting, and I liked what I saw. "Let's get started to see how well-behaved Coco is." Monika invited me to step aside as she took Coco off the leash.

"Oh no! You have to be careful; she won't come back to you!" Even I could hear the anxiety in my voice as I stood on the edge of the fenced-in training area and watched. After a few moments, Monika returned to me with Coco obediently in tow.

"You know," her voice was soft, "I understand that you came to me to seek help for Coco. She's fine." Monika paused.

"Really, I'm here to help you, Lokita, to be a better human companion for Coco." She knew I had been through a lot.

Immediately, I could feel the truth of what she was saying, and I appreciated her insight. Coco and I loved our sessions with her, and she helped us grow as a team.

In terms of my physical health, one remaining issue was that I had severe arthritis in my left knee. As a teenager, I had been the athletic type. My hometown was located between two rivers, and my parents signed me up for training at our local rowing club when

I was 12. Alas, nobody had told them that knee injuries are the most common health problem for rowers—incorrect posture can easily twist the knees—and by the time I was 15, I had to undergo surgery to fix broken cartilage in the joint.

The recovery had been a challenging and formative experience, as I had to walk on crutches for six months and quickly discovered that my heartthrob boyfriend was not the fairy tale prince I had made him out to be. Once I got home from the hospital, he called me "a cripple" and swiftly ended our teenage romance. To top it off, I had to give up sports so that my repaired knee would have the best possible chance for a long and healthy life.

It did pretty well for a few decades, but in recent years had been deteriorating steadily. I was already limping, and sometimes, when nobody was around, even using a cane. I badly needed knee replacement surgery, but I kept on postponing it. Something had always been more important to deal with than my knee. Now I had to face it.

Two months after my arrival in Germany, I consulted an orthopedic surgeon, who left me without doubt about what needed to be done.

"Ja, Frau Carter, you can see here that the bones are rubbing together. There is no more cartilage left in the joint." He showed me the damage on a backlit X-ray screen. "It looks painful and won't improve. A knee prosthesis is needed to restore your quality of life."

I hesitated. "Given my recent chemotherapy, do you think it's advisable to proceed, or should we wait for my immune system to recover?"

The surgeon's response was upbeat. "I've looked at your reports, and I'm confident you can deal with it, both physically and emotionally."

And so, on August 26th, 2016, I had my long overdue knee replacement surgery.

Why did I choose to have this major operation? Why now, after all I had been through? Did I not have enough to endure? My attitude was, "Well, it's a miracle that I'm still alive. And for however long I continue living, I want to live without knee pain and walk properly." I would never be entirely out of the woods with cancer, but I could give myself the best chance to enjoy my life for however long it would last.

Given the extensive recovery time, Monika, the dog psychologist, agreed to take Coco in for a couple of months, and I was free to focus on my surgery.

For the operation, instead of general anesthetic, I had chosen sedation and a spinal tap, numbing the lower half of my body but allowing me to remain conscious, giving me the dubious privilege of hearing the sounds of sawing and hammering as the surgeon removed the damaged area of bone.

Later, when the sedation had worn off, I found myself back in my hospital room, wrapped in the special cozy quilt I had brought to create a comfort zone. A nurse entered the room.

"Hallo, Frau Carter. Everything went very well."

Then I noticed a small gadget in my hand that was attached to my body.

"This is a hand pump," instructed the nurse. "You can squeeze it whenever the discomfort gets too strong, and it'll inject more pain reliever into your system."

I was glad to be in control of dealing with my pain, but to my dismay, no matter how many times I squeezed the pump, it didn't work. As soon as the effect of the spinal tap wore off, I was in agony. Bright yellow stars flashed in front of my eyes whenever I closed them, giving visual expression to the torture in my knee. My face had taken on a deathly pallor, and I came close to passing out.

The doctors were alarmed and puzzled. Maybe my body's resistance to the pain medication was a result of the recent chemo treatment in California? Maybe it was because I had been given morphine during the time of the mouth sores?

Everyone was concerned, kind, and caring, doing whatever they could, but it seemed to take forever until they found the right cocktail of medication to alleviate my acute discomfort. I never want to experience pain like that again as long as I live.

In Germany, knee replacement surgery is typically followed by several weeks in a rehabilitation clinic. The one I chose was located in a popular seaside town close to where I grew up.

I participated in daily sessions of physical therapy and lymphatic massage, enjoyed movement activities in a heated pool, classes where I was taught how to walk with my new prosthetic joint, and exercises to bend and flex the knee to regain mobility.

After my first two weeks there, I received an email from Leon and Aicha, the prosecuting attorneys in Steve's homicide case, confirming that the preliminary hearing was about to begin in Marin County.

At a preliminary hearing, also known as "prelim," the court hears evidence from the prosecution and arguments from defense attorneys to decide if there are sufficient grounds to order a jury trial of the accused. In other words, this was when all the grim details of Steve's killing would be made public.

During the prelim, I had daily email contact with Leon, and at my request, he summarized what happened in court each day. For example, one of the particularly distressing details to emerge was how Steve had driven to the trailhead where the three killers were waiting and watching for a likely victim to rob of their car. The woman, Lila Alligood, said something like, "Yep, that's the one. Let's kill the old man."

I also learned that when Steve was found lying on the ground bleeding, with Coco's leash still clasped in his hand, he was most likely alive for a few minutes rather than dying instantly after being shot. Apparently, he had bled to death slowly.

Those images etched themselves into my brain: my beloved Steve's life slowly draining out of him on the trail, still holding onto his faithful dog, who was wounded and crying, while those drug-crazed killers drove off in our car. Those pictures assaulted me every waking moment and affected my entire experience at the clinic.

In my head, the questions went around and around. "What were his last thoughts? Was he thinking about me? His children? Did he know Coco was shot? Or was there only the realization that he was dying? Or maybe nothing?" These questions and images still haunt me even today, years later.

Because the clinic's internet connection was poor, I couldn't have online meetings with Dr. Matt, my therapist. However, my rehab doctor prescribed daily counselling with a competent psychotherapist at the clinic. She was a godsend, a compassionate fellow human being by my side in the darkness, an angel listening to me as I was overtaken by tsunamis of sorrow, grief, anger, and despair.

When the first anniversary of Steve's murder approached, I was still in rehab. I watched October 5th come closer and closer with trepidation, anticipating a dramatic day with lots of tears and grieving.

By this time, the preliminary hearing had finished. Leon sent me the complete 715-page transcript, and I decided to spend the anniversary reading it. Somehow, I needed to know all the facts.

The computer screen was lit up in front of me for many hours. I pored over pages upon pages describing in great detail who the killers were, what they said and did, what the police saw when they found Steve's body on the trail, and how the suspects were arrested. Everything was contained in this document.

At last, there were answers to many of the questions that had been circulating in my head: "Who found him? Was he still alive? Where did they take his body? What did he say to the killers when he realized they were going to shoot him? What did the murderers do after shooting him?"

I also understood the overall context. They had robbed and killed Audrey in Golden Gate Park, then made a plan to drive to Oregon to start a new life, farming on a remote plot of land belonging to a distant relative of one of the killers. And for that, they needed the perfect car, ideally a station wagon in which they could sleep, just like the car I had bought. Steve died for that car.

When I discussed it with Dr. Matt later, he supported my decision to read the transcript. "I'm a firm believer in truth over comfort," he said. That felt right. It wasn't a comfortable process, but it was the truth.

I can't pinpoint exactly when the turning point came, when I found myself moving from inner darkness toward a lighter state of being, but I know I received inspiration from a most surprising source.

One afternoon, I was walking slowly around the grounds of the clinic on my bright red crutches, enjoying the autumn colors of the foliage and the crisp air of the approaching winter. Flocks of migrating birds danced in the sky as they began their journey southward to warmer realms.

To catch my breath and pay attention to this spectacle of nature, I sat down on a bench with a view across the countryside toward the North Sea, which glinted like a broad stripe of liquid silver in the distance.

After a few minutes, a very old man, probably in his nineties, came shuffling slowly along the path.

"Guten Tag, junge Frau. Good afternoon, young lady. May I join you for a moment?" When I nodded, he sat down next to me.

I turned toward him. His face was wrinkled, his hair thin, almost translucent, and his eyes bright and filled with contentment. I saw a stylish old man giving off an air of enduring vitality and deep peacefulness.

"My name is Mendel," my bench neighbor introduced himself. "Why are you at this clinic?"

"I'm pleased to meet you, Mendel. I'm Lokita." For a moment, I was tempted to dive into my story—the shooting, the husband, the dog, the grief, the cancer. But for some reason, I decided to skip it. Instead, I just said, "I had knee replacement surgery. And you?"

"Well, I'm also here to recover from a knee replacement."

Then Mendel started telling me his story. He was a retired doctor, aged 95, from a town in Southern Germany. Before his knee operation, he had been given a hip replacement and, further back in time, had been through chemotherapy for cancer, not once but twice. His wife had died of cancer a couple of years ago in a particularly painful way, and he missed her so much.

Mendel's story grew longer and longer, with many dramatic twists and turns. Yet there was no self-pity in his voice. He seemed to be at peace with himself and his story.

My stomach was beginning to growl with hunger. It was getting dark and almost time for dinner. I was about to stand up and go, thanking him for telling me about his life, when I was riveted to the bench by his next words.

"As a young man, I was imprisoned and tortured in a Nazi concentration camp. We were liberated at the end of the war. I barely escaped with my life."

My heart broke open for Mendel. All I could do was reach out for his hand and sit by his side in silence.

Listening to this lovely old man, my own story, which I and everyone else had thought was so heavy and horrible—well, I wouldn't say it paled in comparison, but I could see it in a new light.

Each of us has a story. We often get so caught up in our own troubles that we think we are fated to be miserable, dogged by misfortune, that life has betrayed or victimized us—that life is basically unfair. We don't take the time to raise our heads, look around, and see that each person has their share of misfortune. And when we do, compassion for each other and ourselves often becomes the basis for relating.

What impressed me most about Mendel was that despite the adverse circumstances, the so-called tragedies of human life that he had experienced, his innermost being, his center, soul, or spirit, hadn't been dimmed. On the contrary, he was a vibrant human being in an old body who, at the age of 95, still put himself through knee replacement surgery to remain as mobile and healthy as possible.

Mendel touched my heart deeply, and we held hands together on the bench for a long time. My tears were warm and comforting. I felt at peace, and within my heart resonated the quiet hum of deep acceptance.

His story exemplifies how it is possible to live through the most unimaginable nightmare and continue cultivating a sense of joy. To Mendel I'll be forever grateful because he inspired me to discover this truth for myself on my own path of healing and integration.

One more thing I learned at the clinic was that pain is physical, but suffering is psychological and can be overcome. This wasn't new to me as a concept, but to know it to be true—inside my own body and being—was powerful.

I required four months to fully recover from the knee surgery, and I didn't take my first long walk until I was back in Costa Rica. My goal had been this: "On the first day of January 2017, I'm going to walk with Coco all the way from Montezuma to Playa Grande," which was Steve's and my favorite beach, a strenuous five-mile walk that I hadn't been able to do for several years. And yes, I did it. I kept that promise to myself. I was so proud!

My stay at the rehab clinic came to an end. I moved back into my temporary nest near my sister's home and began outpatient physical therapy. Finally, by mid-November, I felt stable enough on my legs to reunite with Coco.

What a wonderful moment when we saw each other! She licked my face and ran around in circles, jumping up and down, sneezing with delight, while I laughed and cried with joy, trying to keep my balance. It was the sweetest reunion, and I got an inkling that I was beginning a new life.

While I chatted with Monika, Coco lay by my side, almost like she had never been away from me.

"Coco did very well. She was sad for the first couple of days after you left, but she perked up and adapted well to her new surroundings." She fit easily into Monika's lifestyle, her dog training groups, and other activities.

We can never figure out what goes on in a dog's mind, but it seems that Coco lives within an energy field of trust that allows her to remain in the here and now without reflecting on the past or worrying about the future. She lives life exactly the way it is and has no intellectual, rational distractions to do otherwise.

With that quality, she continues to be my guiding light, a humble canine spiritual teacher showing me it is possible to enjoy and celebrate life in the wake of incredible trauma and tragedy.

CHAPTER 13

MEMORIAL & MELTDOWN

It was heartbreaking to empty those rooms—a kind of death, a kind of suicide. I was wiping out my personal history, cutting my roots.

As I stood in the kitchen, I was transported back in time. I saw the four of us around the table—Mutti, Vati, Wiebke, and me—sharing a traditional German lunch with *Königsberger Klopse*, meatballs in creamy white caper sauce, my father's favorite.

"Es wird alles aufgegessen! It all must be eaten," he commanded.

"Whether we like the food or not!" I whispered to my sister, stifling a giggle. It was the same ritual every Sunday.

Afterwards, one of us had to help our mother as she stood at the kitchen sink, loudly singing along to popular German music coming from the radio. Our job was to dry the dishes.

"It's your turn!" hissed my sister, nudging me under the table with her knee. She didn't need to tell me. It wasn't our favorite activity, so we religiously kept track of who had to suffer through it.

I couldn't wait to get out of the kitchen. On Sundays, the radio played the music I hated most: German *Volksmusik* from Bavaria, the kind foreigners think is typical German music, with lots of "oompapa oompapa." Mutti loved it! In the meantime, Vati had retired to his favorite La-Z-Boy chair in the living room, enjoying an after-lunch "Schnapps" followed by a nap.

When the dishes were done, I scuttled back to Wiebke's room and sat on the windowsill with her, gossiping about the people who walked below us in the street.

Or we would assemble a complex, 2500-piece jigsaw puzzle while listening to "our kind of music." Mind you, as we got older, our tastes changed. Wiebke listened to ABBA while I was more into Supertramp, The Sweet, and Status Quo. Wiebke and I can laugh about those days now. But back then, we were not laughing.

Sadly, our father had been suffering from Parkinson's Disease for several years, and now, at the age of 79, he could no longer live alone, even with the help of a nursing service that had been assisting him with his daily tasks of showering, dressing, and eating.

It was clear that his move to a nursing home would be permanent, and so we had to fulfill the ancient task of all children—to clear out the family home. For some 55 years our family had lived here on the top floor of a quaint house in the picturesque town of Friedrichstadt in Northern Germany. The apartment was full of history, family memories, and love, stretching back to my early childhood. Closing its doors behind me for the last time was another steppingstone into an unknown identity. Who was I without my past? Already so much had dissolved around me.

When it was done, I booked my flight to California, as I was finally strong enough to hold a memorial service for Steve. My six-month retreat in Germany had been nourishing and healing. Now I was stepping into the spotlight once more. Although I had mentally and emotionally prepared for the return and was looking forward to seeing my friends, I was also fearful and apprehensive. Would I again be cast as "the cancer-stricken widow of slain Steve Carter"? Could I let go of this particular label?

Physically I looked different. Thanks to chemo, my hair color changed from blonde to mouse grey, was curly and cut very short. There were more wrinkles on my face and neck, and I was slimmer, having lost so much weight.

Paradoxically, these past 18 months had made me both softer and stronger. It was a confusing mix. I felt more vibrant and alive now than at any time since I began chemotherapy, but at the same time, completely bereaved and vulnerable.

With assistance from Logan, my housemate and caretaker in Terra Linda, I had been working on where to hold the memorial service. While I was still in Germany, he had helped me rent the Fairfax community church, which seated about 120. But when the service was announced online, we received more attendance requests within an hour than the church could handle.

"We need to find another facility," I told Logan anxiously. We were running out of time. The memorial had been announced for December 10th, close to the Christmas season, and it was already mid-November. Most locations would be booked out.

"Leave it with me, Lokita. I have a feeling I can pull a rabbit out of a hat," Logan assured me confidently.

And so he did. When I saw the photos he sent me, it seemed too good to be true. The facility was a beautiful Spanish Mission-style building with white adobe walls and red-tiled roofs. Steve would have loved it.

It offered a large, multi-purpose hall for 350 people, complete with support from audio and lighting technicians, and a live stream facility that meant that even those far away —including Wiebke and Gerhard in Denmark—would be able to attend live online.

Unity of Marin was located in Novato in Marin County, California. I had never heard of it before and called the rental manager.

"Hello, this is Lokita Carter. I wonder if your facility is available for the evening of December 10th. I need a room for about 350 people," I said.

"Hello, Lokita. Well, we do have a vacancy for that evening after 5 pm," replied a friendly woman, presumably the manager, "May I ask what kind of event this would be?"

"Oh, that's great! It's for the memorial service of my late husband, Steve, who was shot dead in Fairfax last year. You might remember the story."

I could hear her sigh. "Yes, of course. My condolences. And I do remember you as well!"

I then discovered that the facility's manager was Carynne, one of my fellow students in the Spanish class. What a small world! And what a good sign that this was the right place! I booked with her immediately.

Now back in California, everything—the smell of the trees, the bird song in the air, the climate—reminded me of Steve, his murder, of the cancer and the grueling treatment, the pain, the hypodermic needles, the tears, despair, and hopelessness. The sight of the cancer care center hit me deep in the gut. Paul and Mary Alice invited me to stay in their house, where Steve and I had spent the weeks before he was killed, but I couldn't do it.

Nevertheless, I began to prepare myself for the memorial service. It had to be done. After having wrestled with the idea for some time and much deliberation with Dr. Matt, Bebe, and Logan, I finally had accepted that Steve's friends, family, and our Tantric community needed a memorial service to honor Steve and celebrate his life, find closure, and also see me again and reconnect.

With Bebe's expert help, I carefully chose my outfit: a knee-length dress topped with a dark blue woolly poncho Wiebke had gifted me for the occasion, and a crystal mala for a necklace. I wore black pants and knee-high black leather boots and planned to have Coco next to me on a leash during my speech.

Yes, Coco was coming onstage with me, wearing Steve's favorite red bandana around her neck. Everybody knew she was an essential part of the tragedy, yet not many people had actually seen Coco. Whenever Steve and I had taught a workshop or seminar, we left her at home, together with the rest of our pet family, in the care of Omi, our dog sitter.

I wanted to involve all our guests in the memorial service and had invited them to write something about Steve—some anecdote or expression of their love for him—on a piece of paper. As people arrived, all these notes would be collected in a basket by the door.

During the ceremony, I would give that basket to Steve's daughter so that she and her brother, and any future grandchildren, would be able to look at the notes and know that Steve was loved by many, many people.

On the evening of the memorial service, I waited with Bebe in a side room as the hall filled up. Sensing my nervousness, she gave my hand a reassuring squeeze.

"Sweetie, you'll be fine. Those are your friends out there."

The soft chanting of Buddhist mantras played in the background. The lighting in the hall was subdued, and on the left side of the stage, we had created an altar with two photos of Steve, his ashes, some flowers, and a Buddha statue.

A large tapestry that had been displayed in every workshop Steve and I taught formed the backdrop to the ceremony, hanging on the wall at the rear of the stage.

Then I walked with Coco out into the sea of people, all looking at me, and I hoped that nobody could see how shaky my legs were, how fragile and vulnerable I felt. When I passed those sitting in the front row, I felt so much love that I knew everything would be okay. I could do this!

I took my seat among them in the middle of the front row. Behind me sat Cindy from the Marin Humane Society with a bag of treats should Coco need special attention.

Steve's family, who had been so kind to me the entire time while they had gone through hell, were seated in the front row on the other side of the central aisle. Nearby were Steve's childhood friends. Altogether the atmosphere felt secure and solid.

The hall was now full. The music stopped, the lights faded, and the video screen above the stage showed a photo of Steve sitting cross-legged among jungle-like trees in Costa Rica with Coco by his side. A hush fell over the room, and I could hear the rustle of tissues as Steve's recorded voice guided us into the meditation that we had used to begin every workshop.

"Take a deep breath. And then go ahead and create a grounding cord that goes from your tailbone straight down to the center of the planet." The meditation continued for several minutes, and Steve ended it with an image of golden light flowing down our bodies, like taking a shower under a waterfall.

Then it was my turn. I stood and, with Coco, went up the steps to the stage, where a microphone had been centrally placed for the speeches. There was an air of expectancy. For most of the guests, this was the first time they had seen me since the murder and the cancer diagnosis.

"Listening to the meditation, it's like Steve is still here," I began, with a distinctly audible tremble in my voice. I thanked everyone for coming, thanked them for their love and support, and also took time to thank Coco the Wonderdog for insisting on coming with me onstage, which created a ripple of appreciation and laughter through the sympathetic audience.

"I can stand here, smile, and laugh, and at the same time, I'm devastated. I don't know if time will ever change that."

Then I took time to mention the elaborate fantasies shared with me about Steve's death, including his auspicious reincarnation, his messages through psychics, his real-life purpose, what he could teach us from the beyond, and so on forth.

"I don't know any of that to be so," I told the audience. "We have no idea what happens after the physical body dies. What I do know is that there are certain qualities that Steve shared with us that haven't died."

I spoke about his empathy with plants, his ability to help them flourish, and the beautiful gardens he created wherever we lived. I talked about the love Steve carried in his heart and shared with the world through our workshops. I mentioned his commitment to transformation and spiritual growth and our mutual desire to bring as much awareness to each moment of our lives as possible.

Concluding, I said, "We don't know how long our lives are going to continue, so, as a final statement, I wish that the resonance of Steve's melody will stay with all of you forever."

Our friend Dennis and I had compiled a slideshow of Steve's life, gathering photos from Steve's first wife, his children, and his brothers, plus those Steve and I had taken ourselves in recent years.

We journeyed with Steve through a kaleidoscope of his life experiences: as a baby in his mother's arms, as a goofy adolescent, as a young man driving a flashy convertible, later becoming a father, and finally relaxing in a hammock next to me in Costa Rica. As the slideshow came to an end, the chorus of sniffles and sobs reverberating through the room was a testament to the profound loss we all felt together.

Several friends offered tributes after my speech, about half a dozen in all. I remember being particularly touched by a young woman who had trained with Steve and me.

When pointing out Steve's qualities, she lovingly described him as "the remover of obstacles." That was one of his great gifts as a teacher. When participants came to him with their difficulties, he would always manage to find a way to guide them around, through, over, or under the obstacle and into an open sky of new possibilities.

As the tributes ended, I presented the basket of handwritten notes to Steve's daughter, closed the memorial service, and invited the guests to join me in the large breakout room where refreshments were waiting.

This was also the time when many attendees wanted to speak with me and offer a loving hug. Yet it wasn't easy to take all that in. After what felt like three hundred hugs, I noticed Dr. Matt nearby and threaded my way over to him through the throng of people. "Matt, can you please talk to me for a few minutes? I need to have a little break!" He was happy to hold me in his arms, my head nestled against his chest.

Logan was also close by, and for a while, the three of us were in a little bubble together, giving me some quiet time amid all the emotion.

The event was everything I had hoped it would be, and I managed to get through it without breaking down in grief. Curiously, several people told me afterwards that I had appeared to be strong when, in reality, I had been feeling extremely vulnerable the whole time. It became more apparent than ever before that strength and vulnerability are two sides of the same coin.

Eventually, the guests departed, and it was time for me to go home. In the parking lot, some close friends and I stood together for a last chat.

"Thank you all for helping to make this evening so special and sacred." I looked around our small circle, taking in everyone's faces. "Perhaps Steve will have heard the words from your speeches wherever he is now. I'm so grateful for your love and caring."

By now, I was crying, and they huddled around me, holding me close and praising me for my strength and determination. In a couple of days, I would be returning to Costa Rica, and we had to say goodbye for who knows how long. I had reached another milestone.

"Home" for me that evening was a cottage in San Rafael I had rented for a few days since I wasn't living in Terra Linda anymore. It was set in a quiet location and had a small garden. I was looking forward to relaxing there after the intensity and excitement of the memorial service.

It was around eleven o'clock, dark, and quiet by the time I got home. Coco went straight to her bed, and I turned on the heater, took off my outfit, wrapped myself in a cozy woolen robe, and sank into the velvet pillows of the sofa, reflecting on the many moments of the evening. I had completed what needed to be completed.

But the stillness of that moment wasn't what it appeared to be: quiet satisfaction at a task well accomplished. Instead, it was the calm before an unexpected storm. Before I knew what was happening, my body was contracting, my heart was beating furiously, and everything rose from deep within: the pressure from organizing this memorial service, the grief, the horror, the love, the loss, the pain—it all rushed over me like a tidal wave, crushing me.

On my own in an unfamiliar, impersonal house, without any emotional support except Coco, I couldn't calm down, relax, and recover my equilibrium.

The worst was that I couldn't stop blaming myself for Steve's death. I repeated in my mind, over and over, "If only I had gone with him to Bolinas that day…if only I hadn't bought that car…if only I had decided to get the cancer treatment in Mexico like Steve wanted…if only I hadn't contracted cancer…if only I hadn't gone to Harbin for the Watsu training and met Steve…if only I hadn't been born, then Steve would never have married me and died because of me…."

Paul once told me he had suffered similar pangs of regret for telling Steve about the trail where ultimately, he was killed.

I was torturing myself with remorse, self-blame, and guilt, which dragged me into a mental rabbit warren, down complex tunnels that led nowhere, running on and on in pointless yet unstoppable repetition. "If only…if only…if only…."

Having done everything I could for Steve—arranging his cremation, going to court and facing his killers, holding his memorial service—I could now lay down and die. There was nothing more I could do. No future for me. In this moment of great sorrow, I couldn't distance myself from the emotions and the mental drama.

By about 1:00 am, the feeling of suicidal despair became so strong that I decided to call Bebe. It was a cry for help, for a lifeline to prevent me from doing…I don't know what.

It was one of those movie scenes where the main character stands poised on the rampart of a bridge, ready to jump into the icy water below and end it all. Then the music changes as a passerby stops and starts speaking to her. By and by, the stranger talks her back into life.

I dialed Bebe's number. "She would for sure wake up and talk to me," I hoped.

"Hello. Are you okay, Lokita?" Of course, her voice was sleepy.

"No, I'm not okay at all!" I cried. It was hard to get any words out, but I did my best. "Everything is done now. I can't do anything more for Steve. I have done everything I could."

"Shall I come over?"

"No," I said. "It's all finished for me. I don't want to be alive any longer. I have nothing else to live for. What am I going to do now?"

"My love," said Bebe, "you will be okay. You are the strongest woman I have ever met. I'm here with you."

"Thank you. I know. But Steve is not here, and there is nothing more I can do! What else would Steve have wanted me to do? My life is over."

I was crying so hard that it was difficult for her to understand me.

"You have many friends who love you, Lokita. You have Coco. You have your father, sister, niece, and nephew. We are all here for you. You will feel better soon."

"No! Time doesn't heal all wounds," I wailed, "My wounds will never heal. Why did I survive all this? Why can't I just die?"

Bebe was clear and firm, as well as immensely compassionate.

"You can't do this to us, killing yourself; you just can't. It would break all our hearts," said Bebe. "You'll inspire and help many people with your strength and story. It's important for all of us that you stay courageous and alive."

I listened to her words of encouragement. I listened to the love in her voice and her fears for my safety. She had to talk me down off the bridge; eventually, she succeeded. We were on the phone for about two hours as I poured out all my sorrow, grief, and loss.

I wept over my long cancer treatment, Steve's murder, the wounded dog, the knee replacement, and the loss of my childhood home, releasing the flood of emotions I had held back during the memorial service.

I awoke the next morning to find I was still alive. My friend had given me a precious gift: the strength to pass through my darkest night of misery, face all my inner demons, and emerge unscathed in the reassuring light of the following day.

In the hope of bringing a little normalcy to my situation, Bebe took me on a shopping trip that morning, and slowly, slowly, I began to regain a sense of proportion and balance. It was not that I discovered a special reason for living. Instead, what I experienced was that life *is* worth living, regardless of any explanation or cause, simply because that is life's nature.

Life wants to live. Lokita wants to be. And maybe, one day, she will also feel the urge to dance again.

My flight back to Costa Rica was booked for the next day. Arriving home after 16 months would require another round of determination and resolve. Steve's personal belongings, which he had packed away before joining me in California for the cancer treatment, were still there, waiting for my return. All his clothes, tools, car, motorbike, energy, and love we had invested in the property—it was all there to be faced and dealt with. Our home. Forever without Steve.

CHAPTER 14

COSTA RICA BOUND

There is a Zen story about a Japanese mystic who, when asked by disciples to share the secret of his enlightenment, simply replied, "When hungry, I eat; when tired, I sleep."

To me, this story made sense when, after many months, the great drama of Steve's murder and the intensive cancer treatment had passed. In their wake came a quieter, seemingly less eventful time of tidying up loose ends and rediscovering myself. I'd become a one-breasted, cancer-surviving, post-menopausal widow, dealing with the ongoing court proceedings and saying a final goodbye to Steve in a ceremony with his ashes.

It was a period of re-entering ordinary life, but it wasn't without its remarkable moments. For example, not many people fly with their dogs, let alone together inside the cabin.

Traveling on an airplane with a dog from country to country is no simple matter. A so-called pet passport proving the identity of the dog and all its current vaccinations and parasite treatments is the first essential. A health certificate signed by a licensed veterinarian and endorsed by an official government vet has to be issued no more than ten days before the arrival date in the other country. Coco would be in a transport kennel large enough for her to stand up and turn around in, and would fly in a pressurized and climate-controlled area of the plane's luggage hold.

Some years before, when I had travelled with her for the first time, I had been very anxious. Once her kennel had been examined and passed by customs inspectors and Coco was locked inside with a special chewy treat, I had to walk away. I could hear her crying pitifully. The echo-chamber effect of the large airport hall amplified her howling so much that I could still hear it when walking through the security checkpoint.

At the gate, I found myself pacing around, nervously chewing on my nails.

"Is she okay in the kennel? Will she be on the same plane as me for sure? Is she going to come out at the baggage claim belt? No, of course not, so where will I pick her up? What if she was put on the wrong plane?" I fidgeted obsessively with my hair, looking pale and miserable.

A flight attendant approached me with a concerned look on her face.

"You look very upset. What might be the matter? May I help you in any way?"

I told her.

"As a passenger who flies with an animal, you have the right to know that your animal is on board," she reassured me. "When you board the plane, please introduce yourself to the chief flight attendant or the purser, and they will talk to the captain."

As we were taxiing for takeoff, the captain announced, "Ladies and gentlemen, this is your captain speaking. I have good news for Mrs. Carter. Mrs. Carter, your dog Coco is okay. She is on board."

Many passengers erupted into spontaneous applause. I bet the people sitting near me could see from my dark red blush that I was *the* Mrs. Carter! What a moment to have shared with all those strangers.

This time, in December 2016, Coco was allowed to travel with me in the cabin from San Francisco on my journey back to Costa Rica. My therapist had certified Coco as my "psychiatric service animal" because I had post-traumatic stress disorder, which triggered irregular anxiety attacks. The dog was needed to keep me calm.

Coco looked impressive in her special "Service Animal" vest that made it clear she had official authorization to be on board.

There was no way that she would fit under the seat in front of me. Instead, I had reserved a bulkhead with more leg space. Chilled-out Coco sat down on the floor at my feet, but when she lay down and stretched out, her paws touched the feet of the man sitting next to me. I could sense that he didn't particularly like the situation, but thankfully he didn't make an issue out of it.

Passengers from other rows were intrigued and came over. "Isn't that a Doberman? Wow, we have one. Let me get my wife!" There was quite a commotion in the plane's aisle for a few minutes as people lined up to take pictures of Coco in her official service dog vest.

Soon, one of the flight attendants approached and requested that everyone return to their seats as we were preparing for takeoff.

Then, as we were asked to fasten our seatbelts, Coco jumped up on my lap and looked out the window. I had just enough time to memorialize this moment in a photo before all electronic devices had to be turned off.

Returning to Costa Rica was daunting because I was anticipating the brutal emotional impact of missing Steve, knowing he would never be there again. I would get flashbacks, too, about the painful tumor in my breast, once more experiencing that overwhelming feeling of anxiety when I knew something was horribly wrong while being told everything was fine.

Coco, on the other hand, would doubtlessly have a fabulous time because her capacity to live in the present would allow her to enjoy roaming around the garden and playing on the beach, as she had always done.

Upon arriving at San José airport, my fears were confirmed when Leo, our Costa Rican friend and mechanic, met me with our red pickup truck—exactly what I had wanted to avoid. When he had flown to the US to be with me, Steve had left the car with Leo, and I had written to him in advance of my return, requesting that he sell the pickup and buy another car before I got there. I knew that whenever I looked at it, I would burst into tears.

Leo apologized. "I'm sorry, Cariña. I didn't have time. Your new car will be ready next week."

What to do? I could only throw my bags in the pickup and drive it home. My heart grew heavier and heavier the closer we came to Montezuma.

Coco, however, was beyond herself with excitement. I hardly had enough time to open the car door before she jumped out and ran around, rolled on the grass, sniffed everything, and enthusiastically toured the entire perimeter of our two-acre spread, sneezing and barking happily. She knew exactly where she was, and she loved it!

In contrast, I was empty and sad. I sat on a hard wooden chair on the porch, feeling out of place and bewildered by the gorgeous surroundings, the lovely flowers and bushes that Steve had planted, knowing he would never be able to admire how much everything had grown and blossomed. Numbness spread through my body, and I wished everything would magically disappear—the car, the house, the garden, Costa Rica, everything.

Then I heard a little voice. Maybe it was in my heart. Maybe it was coming from the sky. I don't know.

It was Steve. "Thank you for bringing me home," he said.

One day soon, I would create a ceremony with my share of Steve's ashes, bidding him a final farewell in his favorite place. But in the meantime, in the here and now, he was conveying his gratitude to me. A weight lifted, and I could now see the beauty around me.

There were many practical things to be done. I had to sort through Steve's possessions and figure out what to do with them.

I enrolled the help of Bladimir, our 26-year-old gardener, who had been devastated by Steve's death. Steve had been his mentor, his friend, his pseudo-dad, his boss, and his confidant. Bladimir and I had a tearful and happy reunion; we had known each other even before Steve and I built the house. Originally from Nicaragua, he was recommended to us as a gardener in 2005 when he was only 15 years old. I instantly took to him, especially because of his bright smile, sense of humor, and tireless support for my efforts to learn the local language.

I gave most of Steve's clothes to Bladimir to donate to those from his church community who needed them. To this day, my heart misses a beat when I occasionally see someone wearing one of Steve's somewhat unconventional T-shirts.

Some items I selected for Bladimir to keep for himself, such as Steve's baseball caps, a special Panama hat that the two of them loved and had laughed about many times, and a couple of his favorite silk shirts. I knew these things would always be close to Bladimir's heart, and I needed to honor the two men's special relationship in this small yet significant way.

Steve's treasured surfboard was going to belong to a German friend who often went surfing with him.

When I mentioned it to him, he shook his head.

"I can't accept it."

"I'm certain Steve would have wanted you to have it," I assured him. "I'll keep it in the garage, and if you decide you want it, let me know."

Two years later, he called me. "Do you still have the surfboard? Now I feel at peace with Steve's death and can accept it." Grieving has its own timing.

Finally, Leo arrived in Montezuma with my new car and was ready to drive away the red pickup. He was also buying the motorbike Steve had ridden enthusiastically on the dirt roads around our neighborhood.

This was the most challenging moment of all. Giving away Steve's clothes was nothing compared to the car and motorbike.

Through the fog in my tear-filled eyes, I could see the ghost of Steve sitting behind the steering wheel, wearing his surfer dude T-shirt, baggy cargo shorts, and his big smile as if he was still alive.

The worst came when Coco realized what was happening. She jumped up on the bed of the pickup, sat by the motorcycle, wouldn't come down, and even started growling at us.

Coco was a tranquil dog and growled only when there was a good reason, for example, when discovering a rattlesnake or a mountain lion near our former home in California. Now she sat there on the bed of the pickup, growling furiously and showing her teeth.

I somehow managed to pull her off the back of the pickup, but she immediately scrambled under the car and lay there, refusing to move.

The car had a high clearance, so I could crawl underneath, attach a leash to Coco's collar, and drag her out against her fiercest resistance and all the tears, pain, and sorrow in my heart.

Leo drove off, and I wailed until the car disappeared from view. Coco's head hung down as she slouched off to lie under a bush with a depressed look. But after half an hour, she reemerged and bounced back to her usual exuberant self.

A car is just a car until it is not just a car. Things in our lives take on special meaning, and even though, in reality, they are mere "things," we get attached to them. They hold memories, and letting them go can be difficult. This was certainly the case with me. Each item I let go of was a loss, a small moment where grief raised its head, always a reminder that everything is impermanent. Yet at the same time, I knew that clinging to things and circumstances would bring me nothing but suffering.

I kept a large plastic box filled with Steve's clothes and favorite books. Only with time was I able to let more and more of those items go; a T-shirt here, a book there. Eventually, all that was left in the box were his favorite bright blue Guatemalan T-shirt, with a typical indigenous design, his green garden hat, and a turquoise silk dress shirt, hand-painted with lotus blossoms, that we bought during our "honeymoon" at the Bamboo Hut in Hawaii, back in 1998. His scent is long gone, yet I find myself holding these items close to my nose from time to time, remembering how handsome he looked and how happy he was about them. I imagine I'll keep them forever.

As the next step in my new life, I decided that if I was going to continue living in Costa Rica, I had better become visible and get back to socializing and meeting people, this time on my own. Until then, people in our local community had known me as part of a couple, "Steve and Lokita."

When I went shopping in our local town, the Costa Ricans showed me their heartful and matter-of-fact way of accepting death and living with it.

"Oh, Lolita, we're sorry to hear about Steve. That must have been hard for you to lose him. Now he's gone, and we're glad you're still here! Gracias a Dios!"

After that, they would never mention Steve again and related to me as an individual, which I greatly appreciated.

By the way, these locals never called me "Lokita" because, in Spanish, this means "crazy little girl." Instead, out of respect, they called me "Lolita."

Steve and I had known many ex-pat Americans and Europeans who, like us, had fallen in love with the Montezuma area. I decided to invite some of them over, usually one-on-one. We would have a cold drink, tea, or lunch together. In this way, I soon discovered there were many who liked me and whom I could continue to consider my friends, even without Steve.

But these meetings didn't always work out as anticipated.

"Lokita, did you already forgive yourself?" asked someone I had been interested in getting to know better.

I was puzzled. "For what?" I asked.

"We all contribute to the circumstances in our lives, don't we?" he continued.

"Yes, I guess so." I said aloud while silently wondering, "Where is he going with this?"

"Have you forgiven yourself for creating the cancer?"

I was shocked. "The cancer? How would I forgive myself for creating this random, rare cancer?"

"Well, I practice the ancient Hawaiian art of forgiveness as a way to heal. You should forgive yourself for creating the cancer and especially for creating the murder of Steve in your life."

"Let me repeat this so we are both clear that I heard you correctly." I could barely disguise the incredulousness in my voice. "Are you telling me I'm responsible for creating the cancer and Steve's murder in my life?"

"Yes, and you must forgive yourself for it before you can heal."

The easy flow of conversation ended then and there. Eventually, he left, and I never invited him back.

This incident gave me insight. Unless they had experienced such trauma, perhaps it wasn't possible for most people to truly comprehend the pain I had been through, however much they loved and appreciated me.

But some did understand. Near the end of my chemotherapy, an acquaintance visited me in Terra Linda. Taking my limp hand in his warm grasp, he revealed that his brother had been murdered while on vacation in Mexico a few years earlier and that his killers were never found. The tears in his eyes had spoken of his sorrow, deep compassion, and understanding, and I melted into the healing balm of our long embrace and silent connection.

Meanwhile, I had to figure out how to function in the world on my own after 17 years of marriage and come to terms with the reality of property ownership. It was a good first step to make my mark in the garden, even though it had been Steve's pride and joy and at first glance there wasn't all that much that had to be changed.

However, one particular garden path I had always disliked led from the main house to a cabin we occasionally rented out and snaked directly past the floor-to-ceiling window of my office.

My first project with Bladimir was to shift this path. The entire time it took to do this work, I felt almost guilty, knowing that, in some small way, I was destroying Steve's vision for the garden.

Yet I had to let that vision go, and as time passed, I brought more and more of my own flavor to the property, making it my home and claiming sole ownership instead of clinging to the past. The history would always be there, but the property was now mine alone.

I couldn't hold on to Steve by stopping the clock and preserving everything the way he had wanted. Steve would never come back to me, whatever I did. In any case, the plants grew and changed; as they did, so did I.

At times I was confronted by my own irrational reactions when people tried to comfort me by saying, "Steve would have wanted you to be happy and enjoy life."

Paradoxically, such remarks only exacerbated the pain and grief, and I would want to snap at them, "Yes, I know! That's exactly what he would have wanted! But who cares! He's dead! It's over!"

Early in February 2017, a couple of months after arriving in Costa Rica, it was my birthday, and I invited some friends to dinner.

Halfway through the meal, a musical tone on my phone announced a text message. It was from Leon and Aicha, the Marin County prosecutors, requesting a conference call with me.

After excusing myself, I walked into the house and dialed Leon's number.

"Lokita, all three defendants in Steve's murder case have agreed to a plea deal because they want to avoid going to trial." The deal was quite complex, and I listened attentively to ensure I understood. All three had pleaded guilty and many of the charges, like the charge of animal cruelty, were dropped. In return, there would be no trial.

Sean Angold, who had stolen the gun, had agreed to inform on the other two and would receive a prison sentence of 15 years to life, much less than the other two.

Lila Alligood would get 50 years to life. Under normal circumstances, she would be eligible to apply for parole after 85 percent of her sentence had been served, which would be after 42 years. However, since she had been only 18 years old when she committed the crime, her sentence would be reviewed after 25 years under the Youth Offender Parole Program.

The shooter, Morrison Lampley, would get 100 years to life without eligibility to apply for parole until 85 years had been served. However, he would be eligible for a parole hearing after 37 years, at the age of 60, under a different parole program.

"Do you agree to these terms, Lokita?" Leon asked me.

"Yes." Part of me would have liked to compel the three killers to go through a lengthy public trial so they would have to sit on that hard court bench every day for weeks and face the consequences of what they did. I wanted them to be confronted with their senseless actions, to feel shame and perhaps even shreds of remorse. Another part of me simply wanted the whole process to be over.

Leon and Aicha asked me to keep the deal confidential because it hadn't yet been made public. I thanked them and ended the call.

As I walked slowly back to my birthday party, I slipped into that strange space where the apparently solid fabric of reality becomes a fragile illusion. I was balancing between two worlds: the harsh, bleak reality of crime and punishment and the gentle, tropical paradise of life in Costa Rica.

My friends were chatting gaily. I had a nice outfit on for the party, it was a warm tropical evening, and the moonlight reflected as a shimmering ribbon of silver in the ocean. Everything was beautiful, yet here I was, filled with information about a plea deal that would send three people to prison for a very long time for killing my beloved.

My current reality, celebrating with my friends, had nothing to do with court cases and murders, endless cancer treatments, or anything I had been through in California since August 2015. Yet all of that was real as well, and it made my life in Costa Rica seem fragile and precarious, as if, at any moment, the nightmare could come crashing back.

Who was I in all of this? Who was the one witnessing the drama? An ordinary human being, or some kind of spiritual butterfly who needed to pass through many different situations in life to learn the lesson? But what was the lesson?

"Hey, Lokita, where have you been all this time?"

The friendly greeting of one of my guests brought me back to my dinner party. It was time to shrug off the strange feeling and rejoin this pleasant version of reality unfolding in my own home on the occasion of my birthday. So be it. If this was *maya*, illusion, I might as well enjoy it.

When the plea deal went public, Steve's murder became big news again, and several journalists emailed me, asking if I felt justice had been served. After thinking about it a good deal, I concluded that justice could never be served. No punishment could compensate for the taking of human life. Nothing could bring Steve and Audrey back.

Slowly, my life in Costa Rica settled into a new routine. Friends from the US and Germany visited, and I worked with Bladimir in the garden and completed minor construction projects. Coco and I went for daily walks on the beach, and I could sense my health improving every day, bringing vitality and energy back into my exhausted body.

But I also had terrible times when I would cry my eyes out. One particular morning, I woke up feeling sad and lonely, bereaved and miserable, and at the same time, experiencing an urgent need to do something to break out of this endless cycle of grieving.

"Enough is enough!" I told myself loudly. Then, on an impulse, I added, "Look, Lokita, we're going down to the beach now. We're going to take some food, go to Playa Grande with the dog, and stay there until we feel better."

Coco and I remained on the beach for about eight hours. I fixed a hammock between two palm trees so I could lie in it and stare out to sea, giving myself full permission to experience the entire spectrum of emotions: desperation, helplessness, sorrow, loss, anger, and fear.

At the same time, as consciously as possible, I allowed the beauty of nature to permeate every cell of my body. I embraced the natural silence, with no human-created sounds, no noisy machinery, no cars—just the bird calls, the chattering and howling of monkeys in the trees, and the gentle sound of waves breaking along the shoreline. The vitality of untouched, pure nature flowed into me.

I was acutely aware of an invisible clock ticking away the seconds of my life. I didn't know how much time I had left. My chances of surviving the cancer for the first two years after treatment were 35 percent; after that, my odds would improve.

I was faced with this ongoing challenge, not just to overcome the death of my beloved, not just to bid farewell to my former life, but to live now and for the foreseeable future in a state of continuous awareness that cancer could return at any moment and take me away.

By the end of that day on Playa Grande, I was ready to accept the situation. I was more willing to let go of the pain of Steve's absence and embrace living by myself, in my aloneness. I had spent the day amid the hot flames of emotions, and the fire had eventually burned itself out.

One morning shortly after my day on the beach, I got another message from Leon.

"The legal negotiations in the homicide case are finished. The sentencing of Steve's killers is scheduled for April 18th."

"I see. That's good to know."

"Do you think you'll attend the sentencing hearing? This would be your chance to make a victim impact statement in person."

"No! No way!" I wanted to shout. Part of me wanted to turn my back on the past. But in my head, I heard the familiar refrain. *It ain't over til it's over.* I knew I would always regret it if I didn't go. I had to do it for Steve, our family, our friends, the community, and finally, myself.

CHAPTER 15

THE FINAL COURT SCENE

"Hi Greg. I'm flying to California to attend the sentencing hearing next week." Greg was an acquaintance, a retired trial lawyer who lived nearby.

"Wow, that's gutsy of you. How do you feel about it?"

"Actually, I'm nervous because of my victim impact statement." I had been thinking about it a great deal since Leon told me about the April 18th date.

"Well, you're welcome to come over and talk about it." He then had another idea. "Or maybe you want to write something, and we can practice it together. How's that sound?"

"Excellent idea. Thanks. I'll call you when I've got something ready."

Leon had already informed me that, in a rare move, the judge had agreed not only to show the victim impact video I had recorded but also invite me to make a statement in person. I felt it was incumbent on me to do that.

The video contained a strong declaration of how Steve's murder had affected me. In my second opportunity to speak to the court, I wanted to lend my voice to Coco, who was, after all, another victim of their crimes.

Originally, the shooter, Morrison Lampley, had been charged with animal cruelty and first-degree murder. He had put the gun directly to Coco's right eye and pulled the trigger, destroying her eye and shattering the jawbone on the lower left side of her head. Obviously, he was guilty, but in the plea bargain, the charge of animal cruelty had been struck off.

I wanted to make a statement on behalf of Coco. The bullet fired by Lampley certainly impacted her life. She must never chew on a bone again, nor can she play with large dogs because if her artificial jaw breaks in their mock-biting games, it cannot be repaired.

I would stand up and say, "My name is Coco. I'm the dog of Steve Carter, and I was shot in the eye."

After several rounds of practicing by myself, Greg and I met, and when I had completed reading the statement to him, he sat silently for a few moments, then said, "Lokita, it's good, but I've gotta ask you something."

I was surprised and confused by the serious tone of his voice. "Yes, what is it? Don't you like what I said?"

"You did really well, but there are things about life inside prisons that you need to know."

He explained that when convicted criminals arrived at the jail where they would serve their time, they had to show the other inmates their conviction papers, listing the crimes for which they had been sentenced. Depending on the nature of the conviction, they were given a position in the social hierarchy created by the prisoners themselves.

At the bottom of the hierarchy were convicted pedophiles, in danger from the moment they entered prison, exposed to bullying, serious assault, and even death. Prisoners convicted of raping women were also harshly judged and at risk of being beaten or killed.

Another low category was informers, or "snitches," who had made a deal with prosecutors and helped to convict their fellow defendants. Snitches were in constant peril of violence from the general prison population and were often incarcerated in high-security areas for their own protection.

"You may not know, Lokita, that people convicted of cruelty to animals are also considered low on the prison totem pole," Greg explained. "How'd you feel if Lampley was harmed or killed because of what you're saying in court?" He paused and looked at me.

"Remember, whatever you say in court will be all over the media. Everybody'll know. The prisoners all watch TV."

This wasn't something I had considered, and since I didn't say anything but only looked at him pensively, he repeated the question, "If something happened to him, how'd you feel?"

"Well," I said after a moment more, "I'd feel terrible. I really would." He nodded silently.

I took a deep breath. "So I guess I'm going to start afresh."

Discarding that version of my impact statement was the right thing to do, although in the end it didn't save Lampley from receiving a horrendous beating in prison later.

I flew to California a few days before the hearing and rented an apartment near the Civic Center for a week. Wiebke joined me from Denmark to accompany me to court and witness the sentencing.

In the past, I had felt strongly about making court appearances, assuring myself with bravado-filled statements such as, "Yes, sure, I'm going to go. I'm going to give those killers a piece of my mind."

But I had changed a lot in recent months. I was generally a quieter, more reserved person. My mind wasn't working as fast as it once did, and I recognized symptoms of "chemo brain," a common after-effect of chemotherapy that makes thinking slower and somewhat foggy.

Still, I was determined to go through with it. The sentencing marked the end point of the legal proceedings, and it was important to be there.

After Wiebke arrived, one of the first things we did was go shopping. We were looking for something specific—my coat of armor, something to wear to help me feel protected when I stood up and addressed the court. Nothing loose, soft, or flowing would do. I needed to feel safeguarded by what I was wearing.

My intention was to visit one of Marin's glitzy shopping malls, but as Wiebke and I strolled along the Sausalito boardwalk, we passed a women's clothing boutique. Normally, I would never enter, knowing the prices would be prohibitive, but my sister had other ideas.

"Come on, let's go in and have a look at what they've got," she said encouragingly.

There, on the sales rack, was the perfect item: a faux leather jacket in a gorgeous dark red tone. When I slipped it on, there was no question that this was what I would be wearing in court.

On the morning of April 18th, Wiebke and I drove to Marin County Civic Center, greeted Leon and Aicha outside the court, and waited for the drama to begin. The details of the plea deal were known to everyone. The killers were about to be sentenced to a combined total of 165 years in jail.

When we filed into the courtroom, I noticed a substantial police presence at the back of the room—more than before. We were seated in the public section. Steve's family was also present to deliver impact statements, and several of our friends were there in support and perhaps to find some form of closure for themselves. The atmosphere in the room was tense at this stern and serious moment.

The defendants were brought in wearing their prison uniforms, handcuffed, with chains clinking around their feet. To my surprise, they were still looking grungy, pasty, and flabby, as if they were eating too much and not getting any exercise. They sat with their defense attorneys in the same places as before.

Everyone stood up as Judge Simmons entered the courtroom and began the proceedings. Before inviting us to deliver our impact statements, the judge allowed the three defendants to make their own statements to the court, either personally or through their lawyers.

Sean Angold, the informant, remained seated while his attorney stood up and began by expressing concern for his client's safety in prison. He referred to an incident where another of his clients, who had been responsible for the death of a young girl, had been stabbed and killed by other prisoners.

Angold's attorney went on to say that his client had wept throughout the preliminary hearing and was genuinely remorseful for what he had done. He then read out a short, written statement on Angold's behalf.

"I want to express my sorrow at the destruction of two innocent lives and the never-ending pain and anguish the memory of Steve Carter and Audrey Carey will bring and has brought to their loved ones." I didn't believe a single word.

From my vantage point, I closely observed the three defendants. Angold had his head down and didn't look up even once while his statement was read. He seemed to be sniffling, not crying, and I suspected it was an act put on for the court.

Many months earlier, when I had been face-to-face with the defendants for the first time, I tried to get a deeper sense of them, to tune into them intuitively. Angold had immediately struck me as a cowardly type, with a shifty-looking expression on his face, his eyes darting here and there, and his scrunched-up body posture. Back then, I commented to Leon and Aicha, "I think Angold is going to break down and agree to testify against his friends." And so it proved to be.

Next, Lila Alligood's attorney told the court her client had agreed to a sentence of 50 years to life and that she would be filing separately on Alligood's behalf under the Youth Offender Parole program, which offered the possibility of a parole hearing after 25 years of incarceration.

The attorney tried to portray Alligood as having been too young to fully understand the crime she had committed at 18 years of age. Then she announced that Alligood would stand up and read her own statement. She was the only one of the three defendants who did so, and I took my hat off to her for that. Her nose was red, and it was obvious that she had been crying. She seemed genuinely repentant.

"I don't want my words today to cause anyone else any more pain than what my actions have already done. I'd like to say that I truly am sorry. I'm so sorry for what I did and the decisions I made, and the indescribable pain that I caused to others is something I think about every single day, that lives with me in every step that I take. I feel so much guilt and shame for the wrongdoing, the horrible decisions I made, and I'm so sorry. I'm sorry."

Hearing this young woman read her statement broke my heart. She was barely an adult, and now she would spend at least 25, if not 50, years in prison. Steve was dead. Audrey was dead. And here we were, crying for the lives that were lost, including hers.

Then it was the turn of Morrison Lampley's attorney to read out the statement apparently written by his client.

"I wish I could go back in time and change things, but I can't. I know I can never undo the damage. I know I can't ask for your forgiveness, but I hope you can find peace someday."

I had already received his statement in the form of a letter ahead of the sentencing. If I had heard it for the first time then, I might have jumped out of my chair and yelled at him. To my ears, it sounded so devoid of any honest remorse or repentance.

The attorney explained that Lampley had led a life of neglect, abuse, homelessness, and mental illness, as well as being introduced to drugs at an early age. "This information is not offered as an excuse but as an attempt to understand why we are all here dealing with these awful crimes," he concluded.

I watched Lampley as his attorney spoke for him and didn't see any sign of emotion in his expression. He just sat there looking blank, like an empty shell of a human being, as if nobody was home. To me, he was a ruthless, cold-blooded killer without respect for human life, from whom society needed protection.

Then came the victim impact statements. The judge invited me to take a seat in front next to Leon and Aicha. Now, sitting at a right angle to the defendants, I could look directly into their faces and almost touch them. As my video was shown to the court, one could hear a pin drop. People cried behind me. When it was over, I was invited to speak. I made my voice as loud and clear as possible, partly because, in a previous hearing, my friends had commented that I was speaking too quietly, and they had difficulty understanding me.

"What I really would like to do is stand in front of the prisoners and shout and scream and express rage and fury and pain and anger and despair and grief and disgust with my body rather than words, but this is not the right place for that.

"I keep feeling that any moment now, I'll wake up from this nightmare, and Steve and I are together at home with our dog, and that everything is well, and it was just a horrible, horrible dream.

"But it wasn't a dream. This is real. I'm here in this courtroom, looking at Steve's killers. Still can't quite believe it. Sean Angold, Lila Alligood, and Morrison Lampley—many times since you murdered Steve and shot our dog Coco have I wished to be dead. The unbearable grief, the pain and trauma your actions caused me has been just too much.

"But I'm still here. Somehow, I have survived this nightmare. I refuse to be your victim. Me, be the victim of three violent, cold-blooded, evil, braindead drug addicts?"

My body trembled as I spoke, and my hands were wet with perspiration. It was a scary, intense moment, but I had to go on. I had to complete, for my own sake, this strange and terrible relationship that had formed between me and these three people, created by Steve's murder.

"You have taken from me pretty much everything that meant anything to me, but I'm not going to die because of you. Slowly, I'm going to rise like a phoenix from the ashes. I'll live in peace and gratitude for having had 17 wonderful years with a beautiful man in a fun, mature, loving, creative relationship.

"My beloved Steve will forever live on in my heart, and I'll do anything to keep our beautiful dog Coco safe and happy. But you? In a drug-induced craze, you became cold-blooded murderers.

"So now, prepare to pay for it. Your actions cost you your freedom and really, your life. This is your very own horror movie, and it's not going to end any time soon.

"I'm going to walk out of this courtroom later today with a sense of relief that the legal process is over. You, however, will walk out of here to begin your life in hell on earth.

"Will justice be served today when the sentences are handed down? As far as I'm concerned, no punishment, however harsh, could do justice to the horrific, unforgivable crimes you committed—intentionally and without any remorse whatsoever."

I ended my statement and sat down.

Steve's daughter told the court she would be forever haunted by unanswerable questions, such as what might have been her father's last thoughts and how much suffering he endured before dying. She said the murders had robbed her of trust and ease in going about her daily life. "Anyone with dirty clothes and dirty hair is suspect," she said, referring to the rough appearance of the defendants when they had encountered Steve on the trail.

Everyone in the court was touched when she added that one of her chief sorrows was that Steve wouldn't get to meet his future grandchildren, and they would never have the opportunity to meet a wonderful grandfather.

A statement was also read out on behalf of Audrey's family by her aunt, who had travelled from Quebec, Canada, to attend the hearing. She read the statement in French, and Aicha translated it into English. Although I don't speak French, I understood every word.

I continued to watch the defendants as they listened. Lila Alligood's face was contorted in grief and remorse. Sean Angold continued to look down. Morrison Lampley stared straight ahead, expressionless.

As the impact statements ended, I was astonished to realize I felt sorry for the killers. Sorry because they had completely ruined their lives; sorry that their youth had been so difficult that they could feel justified in cold-bloodedly killing two innocent people and shooting a dog; sorry that they would now have to spend a lot of time, if not the rest of their lives, in jail.

Finally, it was time for the sentencing. I was expecting an especially dramatic announcement such as, "Now, will the defendants please rise," as it's often presented on popular TV crime shows. But here, in the reality of the Marin County court, it wasn't like that.

Judge Simmons simply said, "Has everybody completed their statements?"

A silent pause.

"Okay, then. It's time for the sentencing."

She took out a piece of paper and read out the statements: 100 years to life for Lampley, 50 years to life for Alligood, 15 years to life for Angold.

Judge Simmons stood up and left the courtroom. The defendants, who were now convicts, were also led away. The prosecutors and defense attorneys started packing papers into their briefcases. The video screen was taken down, and the public and police began slowly filing out.

I remained sitting with my sister, looking at the scene and thinking, "This movie is over. Finally and completely, this movie is over." It was as if the last scene had been filmed, and the director had called out, "It's a wrap! Thank you, everybody," and now the stagehands were taking down the movie set.

To cap off the surreal moment, as the courtroom emptied, a cleaning lady came in and started mopping the floor.

I scratched my head, saying to myself, "Has this all happened? Has it been real? Or was it just a big film set? What was my role? Who was this character I'd just been playing? And if it's over, who am I now, beyond the drama?"

Outside the courtroom was a crowd of journalists and photographers waiting for interviews. They would want to talk with me. Even before the sentencing, I had wondered if I should face the media this time.

Now I knew it was the right thing to do. The press had been nothing but good to me. They had been kind, compassionate, and clear in their reporting. I owed them the favor.

Leaving the courtroom, I held the arm of my friend Dennis, who was there with his wife, Tracy. We stepped out through the big, brown courtroom doors, and there, as expected, was a sea of reporters.

Camera lights blazed, microphones were thrust in front of me, and the questions kept coming. "Mrs. Carter, what is your reaction to the sentencing? Do you feel good about it? Can you forgive the killers? Do you think justice has been done? Can you tell us more?"

Well, what was I going to say? Did I feel good about it? Did I feel bad about it? I cannot remember exactly what I said, but the main point I emphasized was that no amount of punishment could bring Steve or Audrey back. The sentences couldn't turn back time. The jail terms couldn't take away the pain that I, my family, my friends, and the community had gone through.

Eventually, I was whisked away by a police inspector who wanted to protect me as well as clear the corridor, assuring me, "You've given enough to them, Mrs. Carter."

The journalists were happy. At last, they had some good footage of me, showing their viewers how I looked and talked.

Dennis escorted me out through the doors of the Civic Center, and there were my friends, waiting for me. I hugged and thanked each one of them. Many hadn't seen me in a while and were happy to see that I was healthy and looked good.

Then Wiebke and I got into our rental car, drove to Sausalito, and walked down to the waterfront. On a whim, we bought ourselves two delicious ice cream cones.

We sat on a wooden bench, enjoying the warm spring sunshine, the water lapping against the edge of the wharf, the seabirds screeching as they glided overhead, the people walking by. That was a big moment for both of us. We were reminding each other what normal life can be like, reclaiming our right to be ordinary and happy with the simple things—like ice cream.

Wiebke and I spent two more days together, and then I flew back to Costa Rica.

After the sentencing, it was time for the three convicted murderers to leave Marin County Jail, where they had been held since their arrest on October 7th and commence their prison life in other institutions.

Lila Alligood was sent to the Central California Women's Facility in Chowchilla.

The two men were transferred to San Quentin, California's oldest men's state prison that, among other population, housed those on death row. In this part of the legal procedure, sentenced male prisoners would spend a maximum of 30 days in San Quentin to get assessed, psychologically and physically—for potential violence and possible flight risk—and then be transferred to the correctional institution where they would serve out their time.

From San Quentin, Sean Angold was sent to the High Desert State Prison in Leavitt, a maximum-security jail where he needed to be kept more or less in solitary confinement for his own protection.

He was a snitch who had ratted on his friends, making him a target for other prisoners.

Leon told me it was possible to check on the prisoners via an Inmate Locator app online, and when I did so, I was surprised to see that, a couple of months later, Morrison Lampley was still in San Quentin.

When I asked Leon why he had been there so long, he explained that soon after his arrival, Lampley was beaten by two prisoners who, like him, were passing through the 30-day assessment period. His jaw was broken in many places, so much so that he had to be kept in the prison hospital. His injuries were very similar to those his shooting had caused Coco.

Those two inmates got another two years extra on top of their existing prison sentences for the assault on Lampley, but presumably, according to the strange code set by the community of prisoners, their standing in the social hierarchy went up, having beaten a man who shot a dog and turned a cancer-stricken woman into a widow. Lampley was eventually sent to a jail in Southern California, where they placed him in a substance abuse treatment facility.

A crime reporter for the San Francisco Chronicle, Vivian Ho, wrote an investigative book entitled *Those Who Wander: America's Lost Street Kids*. She revealed that she had visited Lampley in jail several times to talk to him and that she had expected him to repent for the killings. He never did.

She added, "The only regret of his that I believed to be real was that Steve's dog Coco had gotten hit in the shooting and lost an eye. 'I've been abused by humans my whole life,' he said. 'People who have been abused, we connect with animals who have been abused. I'm never going to get over the fact that Coco got shot in all that.'"

Since the murder and facing the killers in court, I never expected them to repent because that expectation would have resulted only in disappointment. There was nothing I could do to change them. I couldn't make them feel remorseful. They were who they were. They did what they did. And really, it didn't matter to me whether they regretted their actions or not. It wouldn't have made a difference anyway.

In the first couple of years after Steve's murder, I was often asked if I had forgiven them, with the subtext that unless I had done that, I could never be free to continue living without that weight on my shoulders. To forgive means to let go of resentments, thoughts of revenge, and anger. It also means cultivating a feeling of understanding and compassion for others.

Forgiving is not something I decided to do one day, perhaps with a little ritual, "Now I forgive them and move on." It has been a gradual process of allowing my attachment to emotions like rage and fury to fall away. To notice such emotions and not feed them has been the key. It takes a lot of energy to continue feeling angry or plot revenge and gives only brief mental gratification.

Feeling compassion opens the heart. That said, the only compassion I ever felt was for Lila Alligood when she cried in court and later for Lampley after I was told he had been beaten in prison. Perhaps feeling compassion then was the first step toward forgiveness. Mind you, I never felt a shred of compassion for Angold, who had stolen the gun.

Many people suffer from abuse, mental illness, and drug addiction, but that does not give anyone a license to kill others.

In the end, my very best was to give the three of them a *namaste*, acknowledge the divine essence that lies at the heart of every human being, leave them to their destiny, and move on.

CHAPTER 16

HAPPY ENDINGS

In embracing the spiritual vision of Tantra, I accept life in its totality—the good with the bad, the living with the dying, the highs with the lows, the long summer days with the cold winter nights.

It's a holistic vision in which, essentially, we are choiceless. Just by being born, we receive the whole spectrum of human experience, and we are as bound to the natural laws of existence as the swallows who fly south to follow the sun and the wild geese who fly north to nest and feed.

But, as a wise man once said to me with a smile and a chuckle, "Yes, we are basically choiceless, but it's okay to have preferences!"

It's my preference to give this book a happy ending. In fact, not just one happy ending, but two. This is not something forced or artificial. Instead, it reflects my own experience that life gives us the power to be joyful, even after tragedy.

The first happy ending concerns the Marin Humane Society, which had poured so much time, love, and care into saving Coco's life and, through her, my own life. Not only did it cost them some

$40,000 to rescue her and heal her wounds, but they also gave their services freely, without passing the bill to me.

So, when Cindy asked me if I would agree to participate in a short film about saving Coco, I readily agreed. She explained that their society held an annual fundraising gala, and they planned to show the video about Coco in March 2018.

I'm not shy in front of cameras; in fact, I was looking forward to it. We made a date to do the filming a couple of days after the sentencing, when my sister was still with me. I set aside a whole day and drove to the offices of the Marin Humane Society, located in a leafy setting in Novato.

We were welcomed warmly, and I was ushered into a side room for makeup. I had already chosen what I would wear—a gray sweater and my maroon-colored faux leather jacket, my so-called "coat of armor" that I had worn at the sentencing hearing, only this time there was no need for protection. I just really liked the jacket!

As I saw myself in the mirror while basic makeup was applied to my face, I reckoned I looked good. My hair was short, slowly growing back after chemotherapy, but also quite stylish. Even though I felt fragile, I was confident I could make a good impression.

One large room had been converted into a studio for the occasion, and there was a film crew plus their equipment—lights, cameras, and microphones. I was introduced to the movie director, Mario, a young videographer, by chance from Costa Rica, who would be interviewing me.

We sat down in comfortable chairs, the cue was given, the cameras started rolling, and I was invited to retell the whole story: who I was, how I felt when I saw Coco for the first time as a puppy, what happened to Steve, how Marin Humane Society saved our dog, how Coco then saved my life by giving me hope and inspiration, and so on.

Although my voice was wobbly with emotion, I was happy to share my story, knowing that it might help many animals in need and perhaps their human companions at some future point.

Naturally, no movie about Coco would be complete without plenty of footage of Coco herself. Three months later, I was able to bring her to California.

Coco and I accompanied the film crew to Muir Beach, where I played with her on the sand, taking her for a walk and allowing her to jump up on me. We also reenacted some of the more dramatic moments in the saga, such as having Coco lie down on a hospital bed as if she was still recovering.

Early the following year, I received an invitation from Cindy to the society's annual fundraising gala, to be held on March 10th, 2018. Incidentally, that would have been our 19th wedding anniversary.

Of course, Coco was invited too, but since I was only going to be in the US for a few days to attend the gala and support the fundraising efforts, there wasn't enough time to gather all the necessary documentation for her return travel. Cindy was disappointed, but she understood.

The gala was held at a luxurious venue in Marin. There were about 350 guests, all glamorously dressed for the occasion, and it was obvious that this was a big deal socially, with many wealthy and well-known people gathering for the annual event.

A delicious, multi-course dinner was served, and everybody talked, drank, ate, and enjoyed themselves. I sat with Cindy and the team from the Marin Humane Society at a large round table decorated with an impressive bouquet of flowers, candles, and fine china.

The video was slated to be shown after the meal on the venue's huge cinema-style screen, and everyone had a ringside seat.

Because Coco had been part of the homicide investigation, no details about her rescue and survival had been made public until the sentencing. Even then, the media focused on the big news—the lengthy jail terms given to the killers. Therefore, none of the guests at the gala knew the inside story or the Marin Humane Society's role in the drama.

"Saving Coco" was just under seven minutes long and had been beautifully compiled. The movie began with photos of Steve and me while I talked about our 17 years together. Then I described how Steve had wanted a guard dog, was insistent that it had to be a Doberman, and how we visited a litter of recently born puppies to choose the brown, golden-eyed Coco with the huge, soft paws.

Steve had picked out a small, brown female. "She and Steve looked into each other's eyes, and it was love at first sight," I recalled, adding jokingly, "She was really Steve's other wife!"

There were photos of Steve and Coco walking on the beach, playing together, and having a great time. "Everything was just wonderful for them," I related.

Then came the tragic moment on October 5th, 2015, when Steve was killed and Coco badly wounded. I talked about our last moments together, Steve's text message that they would be home soon, waking up in the night to find them missing, and the arrival of the police with their awful news.

The movie described the emergency medical treatment needed to save Coco, with a gripping account by Elisa Bowyer, one of Marin Humane Society's veterinary doctors, combined with graphic photos of Coco's injuries.

Reflecting on Marin Humane Society's efforts, Cindy, with tears in her eyes, said, "It was too late for Steve, but just the beginning for Coco." She was aware that it wasn't only Coco she was trying to save but her owner as well. "Because battling cancer's not easy, and getting bad news about your dog, on top of the death of your husband…I couldn't imagine doing that myself."

"To be able to give to someone who is really struggling was one of the best things I've done in my career," she added.

The movie ended with our scenes from the beach, showing Coco and me playing and enjoying each other's company. "I really didn't want to live, but everything changed because Coco came back to me," I explained. "For that, I'll be grateful until my very last breath."

This short but intense movie took the gala guests completely by surprise. They had no idea what they were about to see, perhaps imagining that they would be viewing a tasteful and inspiring appeal for funds. And suddenly, they realized they were watching a missing chapter in the huge story about Steve's murder that dominated the news channels for the previous two-and-a-half years.

Only now did they realize that the Marin Humane Society to which they donated had saved this dog. From where I was sitting, I could see people starting to cry. Some had their mouths open in astonishment, and others shook their heads in disbelief.

When the film was over, the room became hushed, and time stood still. Nobody knew what would come next. As I walked onto the stage to give a speech, I could see the amazement in people's eyes that the woman in the movie, Lokita Carter, widow of the tragically killed Steve Carter and survivor of life-threatening cancer, was here, in the room with them.

"I'm beyond grateful to you all. Without you, I wouldn't be standing here today. You saved my life with your generous donations to Marin Humane Society." Slowly, I looked around at the sea of astonished, admiring faces. "I'm deeply touched to be here with you, knowing that you've made it possible for Coco to be saved. Through that, you helped me survive."

I also spoke about the bigger picture, about the importance of animals as a healing, supportive, and loving presence in our lives. At the end, I just said, "Thank you."

Spontaneously, everybody rose to their feet and applauded. People clapped for a long time while I held onto my composure for dear life.

Eventually, the guests sat down and began offering their donations for the Fund-a-Need program. Somebody shouted, "I pledge $25,000!" and somebody else announced, "I pledge $10,000!" And so it continued.

Before we knew it, the Marin Humane Society had received more pledges and donations than at any of their past fundraising galas. By making the video and being there at the gala, I could express my gratitude and, in a small way, give back to this organization that had been so incredibly generous to me, with a team so full of love and compassion.

The second happy ending happened at the ceremony I created with Steve's ashes. After the sentencing in April 2017, I returned to Costa Rica, knowing I had faced pretty much everything there was to face—the cancer treatment, the homicide case, the memorial service for Steve, and the sentencing of the killers.

There was only one thing left: to release Steve's ashes into the sea. I had decided earlier that the best day to do so would be his birthday, April 25th, a few days after my return.

I wasn't sure what would happen that day, but I knew it wouldn't be a big gathering since I still felt quite fragile, and another large memorial service with our local friends and community would have been too emotional.

Steve and I had a neighbor called Bee, whom we had known for at least eight years, and whom Steve liked very much. When he had first met her, I was in California, and I remember him telling me on the telephone, "I met a most beautiful woman today. She's my age, has long gray hair, a big smile, and the most beautiful shiny eyes. She's going to be our neighbor with her husband, Mike. You're just going to love her."

Steve was right. Bee and I liked each other immediately. She became my rock when I returned to Costa Rica with Coco after Steve died. Bee and her husband had been deeply affected by Steve's death and missed him dearly. Every time we met, they knew exactly what to say to me at exactly the right time.

Bee and I exercised together, went for long walks with our dogs, drank endless cups of tea, and shared meals. Our friendship continues to this day.

When considering what kind of send-off I wanted to give Steve, Bee came to mind, and so I called her.

"Look, Bee, I have an idea. I want to go with you to Playa Grande, take our dogs, walk the entire way along the edge of the ocean and release Steve's ashes together, just you and me. Steve loved you from the first moment he saw you. I also love you, and I cannot imagine a better person to commemorate Steve's departure with than you. Would you be willing to come with me?"

"Yes, I'd be honored to do that and will gladly come," Bee replied.

We prepared by gathering Steve's favorite flowers from our garden, such as big, beautiful hibiscus blossoms with their long pink stems, ylang-ylang flowers with a strong fragrance, and petals from the pink frangipani trees, as well as several large, flat green leaves and palm fronds.

On the morning of April 25th, Bee and I drove to Montezuma bright and early with our collection of offerings and Steve's ashes.

It's a picturesque, 45-minute walk to Playa Grande, and the path is a complex, windy affair. First, you walk along the beach, then up a narrow path over a hill where you have to scramble over rocks and through crevices. Then comes a waterfall, another beach with rocks, and a shady walk through the jungle, past a fallen trunk, a huge rock, and an area with tall tropical trees.

Eventually, Bee and I came to the end of the path. All along to our left was an endless cliff top covered with ferns, lush foliage, and palm trees, with no houses in sight. Directly in front of us lay a mile and a half of untouched, unspoiled beach, lapped by gentle, turquoise ocean waves in which we could see the silver glints of countless darting fish.

This was a place Steve and I had always loved. We had wonderful times there. This was where I chose to release him into the sea.

"Bee, I'd love to distribute the ashes along the whole beach rather than in one particular spot."

She smiled. "Sure, let's do that."

We were quite spontaneous in how we let go of the ashes. For example, we would take a little bit of ash, scatter it on top of a leaf and then float the leaf on the surface of the ocean, just beyond the breakers, sending a blessing to Steve. "May you be at peace, beloved."

On that day, it was relatively calm and low tide, so we could watch the leaf drifting out to sea.

We used the ashes to write messages like "You're my hero" or "We love you forever, Steve" on the sand and draw hearts around them. The ashes were a light shade of gray-white, and the sand on Playa Grande is a dark, grayish color, which made a beautiful contrast. We could see our messages and symbols as if they were written with a white pen on a dark piece of paper. Then we would watch as a wave came in and washed the message away.

In this manner, we made our way along the entire length of the deserted beach. Sometimes we would just throw a flower into the sea and say things to Steve like, "May your spirit be in a sacred place!" and, "Thank you, Steve, for everything you've given to us. We love you, and the love is never-ending."

Coco skipped playfully along with her two canine friends, Bee's dogs, who all knew each other.

While I was in the mood for ceremony and ritual, occasional silliness crept in, and our farewell became a sacred yet lighthearted affair. I don't believe we must always be in a somber, dark mood to say goodbye to a loved one. The cremation in Marin, of course, had a much more serious and formal atmosphere, but now we could say goodbye with a lighter heart.

Lightness of spirit is a good thing. It was also tinged with sadness because this was the final moment when the ashes would disappear. But overall, it was a moment of gratitude, joy, and love.

Then we came to the end of the beach, where Steve and I had often frolicked. Sometimes we had made love; sometimes we had rubbed each other's bodies with the fine dark sand, giving each other exfoliation treatments.

It was very private, with only the birds, the ocean, the tree-clad cliffs, and the calls of howler monkeys in the nearby jungle. In such an isolated spot, one could easily feel at liberty to do things one might not normally do in public. It was where Steve and I shared so much bliss from the very first time we came here.

Because I had planned to conclude our send-off here, at the end of the beach, I had made sure I had a little bit of ash to release into the sea by myself. Bee was fine with that. In keeping with Steve's and my tradition, I took off my bikini. The bikini was all I had been wearing because it was a very warm April day.

I took the ashes, stood in the surf close to the beach, and rubbed some onto my naked chest, my heart chakra, my third eye, and between my eyebrows. I rubbed the last bit on Coco, standing in the shallow water next to me. After all, Coco had been part of this whole saga.

We went out a little further into the ocean. The water was warm, and my feet and legs were immersed in millions of bubbles sparkling in the sunshine. Steve and I would often run into this white, frothing surf that was so invigorating, lie down and shout to each other, "Champagne! Champagne!" and laugh like children, throwing our arms and legs around in ecstasy.

I walked into the bubbling surf and played with Coco, watching as the waves washed Steve's ashes from our bodies. My tears of sadness, gratitude, and joy flowed freely and became one with the ocean.

Suddenly, something made me look back toward the shore, and I noticed one of Bee's dogs, who had followed us into the water, dashing toward the beach, ears flying.

I turned around…too late! A huge wave was coming at me out of nowhere, toppling Coco and me over. We got completely wiped out and rolled over and over in the surf. It took me a few seconds to find out which way was up and stand on my feet again.

The wave crashed on the beach, swooshing up to Bee's rock. I saw her grabbing our belongings in an effort to save them.

Once the wave subsided, Coco and I walked out of the surf and over to Bee.

"Wow, that was quite the wave!" I exclaimed.

Bee nodded. "Yes, I'm glad I managed to save the bags because I know you have your phone in yours."

Coco was shaking the water off her back the way all dogs do, her ears flapping wildly as she spun her head and body from side to side. I was dripping wet and stark naked.

After my skin had dried a little, Bee asked, "Are you ready to go?"

"Yes, I'm ready. Where's my bikini?" I asked.

"Your bikini? I don't know," she replied, looking in our bags. "It's not here."

"Didn't you pick it up?"

"I don't think so."

"Well, we'd better look for it."

We searched everywhere—in the water, on the sand, between the rocks, and higher up on the beach. Eventually, we found the bikini top but couldn't find the bottom. I had no other clothes and just stood there, wondering what to do.

Then the humor of the situation struck me. I cannot remember if I laughed out loud, but I certainly giggled inside. It was hilarious because I had the strongest intuition that Steve had stolen my bikini bottom!

He was determined to have the last laugh. It felt like his playful way of reminding me of our previous meetings in this spot and our long journey together, beginning with our passionate honeymoon and spreading far and wide as we taught workshops and retreats, sharing the secrets of blissful union.

At the same time, he was saying to me, "Okay, now go on. Enjoy life without your bikini bottom! You're free, you're beautiful, and your whole life is ahead of you."

Fortunately, on a practical level, Bee had a scarf just about long enough for me to wrap around my hips and cover my bottom, so we could walk back to Montezuma, pick up the car, and drive home.

That was my farewell ceremony for Steve, and I imagine he liked it. Since he had never given me instructions for his funeral, it had become my sacred task to create a ritual from my understanding of what would feel best for us both. To say farewell in the ocean, among the waves, felt befitting to our relationship and love.

And sometimes, when I'm sitting by myself, gazing out across a calm ocean, and when that calmness is also reflected inside of me, I can look back at the great drama of my life and catch a glimpse of it as *Leela*, the divine play. I'm able to embrace the theatre of it, the dance of those apparently opposing forces—life and death, love and hate, tragedy and triumph, tears and laughter—and see beyond them to the divine mystery that sustains me and the unchanging essence of who I truly am.

EPILOGUE

Eight years ago, I had aggressive, life-threatening cancer, Steve was killed, and I was in hell. Time and again, people have told me how amazing it is that I have come through these tragic times, I am still alive today, and I am happy. They ask me how I did it. They say I'm the strongest person they have ever met, and they cannot even begin to imagine the pain and sorrow I have experienced. Someone commented that I seem to have regained my faith in life. Truthfully, I never lost it, even when things got very, very difficult.

Actually, instead of faith, I prefer the word trust. Trust has guided me throughout my entire life. Sometimes trust is used to describe positive thinking. "I trust that life has presented me with what I need to grow, that life has not given me more than I can handle."

The trust I'm talking about, however, is more of an unconditional surrender, giving myself to whatever life brings, with no philosophical frame or preconceived ideas. Rather, I accept the circumstances that arise every moment and use my mental and emotional faculties as consciously as possible to decide how to best navigate my way.

Even in moments of anguish, grief, and shock, filled with an acute desire to die and knowing that cancer might get me in the end, I practiced this kind of trust. If that was to be so, so be it. *Que sera, sera.*

Throughout the entire timespan of this story, I have been close to Steve's family. We have visited each other, cried, exchanged emails, talked, and helped each other through the difficult times. I love them dearly, and we stay connected.

Since the mastectomy in December 2015, I have been free of cancer, but this does not mean I'm permanently "cured." The cancer that took my breast has a high recurrence rate, and the usual five-year milestone one hears about does not apply. Hence, I'm especially grateful for each moment life chooses to give me. My body is strong and healthy, I exercise regularly and eat well, and I enjoy each day as a gift from the Divine Mystery.

Yet there are constant reminders that I am living on the edge, balanced precariously between life and death. As soon as I notice anything that could be construed as a symptom, my mind springs into action. A persisting cough could be an early warning of lung cancer, a strange pain in my legs could be the beginning of bone metastasis.

In terms of monitoring for recurrence, I have ultrasound exams on both sides of my chest every six months and an annual mammogram of the right breast. In 2018, there was a brief scare, but it turned out to be a benign cyst that has not changed since then. My oncologist has advised me to return to her only if I detect any symptoms, which thankfully has not been the case.

In many ways, I have changed. Before cancer, I could easily "multi-task" and accomplish many things at the same time, whereas now I function more effectively by focusing on one task at a time, taking it more slowly.

Now, as soon as anything potentially stressful begins to happen, my body starts crying. This is a valuable indicator because even if my rational mind does not recognize or denies the oncoming stress, my body responds with its intrinsic wisdom. I have learned that at such times I need to stop, listen to its messages, and change my behavior accordingly.

The cancer had other effects I hadn't anticipated. Before cancer, I still had, at age 52, regular menstruation. My hormones were alive and well. My menstrual cycles stopped with the first chemo infusion, and menopause began instantly. There was no transitional phase marked by hot flashes, mood swings, or irregular periods that one would normally associate with menopause, through which one could slowly become accustomed to this potentially significant change. From the beginning of the cancer treatment, it took about a year for me to realize what had happened, that another essential part of me had dissolved. Now I discover myself anew in this new "crone" phase of my life.

Coco, my beloved *doghter*, is almost twelve years old, and since the average lifespan of a female Doberman Pinscher is between 10 to 13 years, she is in the later part of her life yet still full of zest, joy, and energy. I'm hopeful that she, the true Wonderdog, will stay with me for at least another five years. She has been such a precious friend and essential to my recovery. Right now, I cannot imagine life without her. That said, I would not want her to outlive me. Coco has been through so much; it would break my heart to think she would have to grieve for me as well.

When Steve was killed, I was certain I would never teach Tantra again, but one day I remembered that I had been a *Tantrika* before I met him and will continue to be so until I die. With this in mind, I started offering exclusive Tantra coaching retreats for couples, which has been very rewarding. I taught a couple of group workshops before the Coronavirus pandemic put a temporary end to it all. It's a joy to work with people, share my understanding, and witness the transformative power of Tantra in action. I often feel Steve's presence in the teaching, and in that way, he lives on, not just for me but for everyone whose life I'm privileged to touch with our work.

All the friends mentioned in this book are still my friends. We are in regular touch and see each other on occasion. I'm grateful to them for their love and precious time sharing our lives. My online blog has helped me stay in contact with my community, and it's a real blessing to feel a strong heart connection with so many wonderful people.

Lately, the profound pull of my homeland called me to spend more time on my home turf in Northern Germany, on the island of Sylt, with my family in Southern Denmark, and with old friends.

By the grace of the Divine Mystery, I'm still alive, and the doors to the next phase of my life have opened and given way to a new perspective, possibilities, and priorities. As much as I venture forward with enthusiasm, I'm forever changed by the experiences I share in this book. Steve's death and my near-death experience have profoundly impacted my life.

Grief is a verb, a continuum, and missing Steve has become part of my everyday experience. The sorrow of losing him, the love of my life, will never end, and there won't be a sudden point of closure. Yet as much as I grieve and occasionally become sentimental and nostalgic, life, as if by some miracle, goes on and continues without him. His love and presence live on in my heart. In the Mexican tradition, they say that the person is dead only when nobody thinks of them anymore. With Steve, that will take a very long time.

I'd like to conclude with this thought:

There is a significant difference between the notions of "letting go" and "dissolution." For example, Steve and I decided to let go of our home and business to move to Costa Rica for a simpler, more laid-back lifestyle. In this context, letting go implied that we actively chose to make those changes. We prepared for them and enacted them.

Cancer and Steve's murder, however, ripped my life apart unexpectedly and involuntarily. Together, those events presented what I came to call the Great Dissolution, a form of psychological death, as my self-image and sense of identity disintegrated before my eyes.

I was reborn with new inner freedom and created a new life for myself, eventually feeling happy and fulfilled again.

Choose wisely how you want to live, and never hold onto anything. Everything is impermanent. What we can take with us when we die is love.

ACKNOWLEDGMENTS

Gratitude is my daily practice. When I open my eyes upon waking in the morning, I'm grateful for seeing the light, for taking another breath, and for the life force that mysteriously flows through me. I'm grateful for my own strength to birth this book. May it bring hope, inspiration, and maybe even a fresh outlook on life to its readers and shine light on their paths.

My love goes out especially to Isabelle, the mother of Audrey who was murdered a couple of days before Steve, by the same three killers. The loss will always be unfathomable.

From the bottom of my heart, I'd like to thank everyone who stood by me during the years when this story actually happened. It is because of the power of your love, generosity, and presence that I am still here.

My heartfelt thanks go to my writer friend Subhuti. His enthusiasm for my story, coupled with his patience, creativity, and gentle guidance made the writing process a deeply healing journey.

I'm grateful to my beta readers for their time and feedback, especially to my friends Tracy and Logan who both read several drafts of the manuscript, brought continuity and consistency to the writing in the early stages, and gave me the courage to persevere through moments of doubt and despair.

Thank you to editor Lia Ottaviano for her content suggestions and keen eye for detail. Thanks to photographer *extraordinaire* Joachim Gern for all the fun and the lovely images, and to Stephan Schaefer for his photo of Coco and me on our favorite beach in Costa Rica. Thanks also goes to Lois Hoffman of The Happy Self-Publisher for helping to bring this book out into the world, and to Daniel Möhrke of Recording Sylt for his technical know-how, and for crying and laughing with me as we recorded the audiobook together.

Deep appreciation is due to my medical team for their expertise and dedication. You saved my life under extraordinary circumstances, even when I insisted that you consider information from a social media platform as a potential treatment option.

My immense gratitude for rescuing Coco goes to my angel, Cindy Machado, to her team at the Marin Humane Society, and to its generous donors, as well as to the medical specialists at the Pet Emergency & Specialty Center of Marin and the UC Davis Veterinary Hospital. Your work, commitment, and passion are astounding.

The prosecution team of the Marin County District Attorney's office, led by Leon Kousharian and Aicha Mievis, has been the kindest, most empathic ally anyone in my situation could ever hope for. I cannot thank you enough for convicting Steve's murderers for their crimes, as well as for your continued friendship. Thank you for reading several versions of the manuscript to ensure the accuracy of the legal proceedings and related terminology, for cheering me on during the writing process, and for believing in me.

I'm infinitely grateful to my psychotherapist, Dr. Matt, who accompanied me with his wisdom, deep understanding, love, and compassion for six years on my journey from the unbearable darkness into the light of life. May you be blessed on your path as you have blessed mine.

Special gratitude goes the team at Spirit Rock Meditation Center, particularly to Jack Kornfield and Mark Coleman for your love and compassion.

Thank you also to our Tantric community. Being connected with you reminded me of the greater whole when everything else around me slowly disintegrated. And to the known and unknown donors who made it possible for me not to have to worry about finances during these darkest times—thank you.

Dearest Christina, Diego, and Rutherford: Our long friendship will always hold a special place in my heart.

My love and profound respect go to Steve's family for being my family, too. We grew closer in our shared ordeal, and for that I am so thankful.

My heart overflows with gratitude for my sister Wiebke and her husband Gerhard, my closest friends Bebe and Benny, Dennis and Tracy, Logan, Paul and Mary Alice, and Roger. Thank you all for holding me safe in the warm embrace of your love. You were deeply concerned about whether I would overcome the cancer beast, and then tragically, you lost a wonderful brother and friend in Steve. To have been supported by you all in your own time of fear and grieving is a priceless gift that I shall cherish to my very last breath.

And Coco the Wonderdog, my ever loyal and loving canine companion, your joie de vivre brings sunshine and positivity to my every moment. You saved my life.

And you, Steve, my love. Thank you for sharing 17 years of lifetime with me. Thank you for the love that lives on long after your death.

ABOUT THE AUTHOR

Lokita Carter, originally from a small town in Northern Germany, embarked on a spiritual quest that led her to Berlin, an ashram in India, and Australia before she met Steve, the love of her life, in a hot springs pool in Northern California in 1998.

Lokita and Steve established themselves as the leading Tantra teachers in the United States. For 16 years they taught hundreds of seminars, with tens of thousands of participants, at respected educational organizations both in the US and internationally.

After being diagnosed with rare, life-threatening cancer, Lokita began a blog documenting her experiences with the illness and intense chemotherapy. Her intention was to create a guide for couples facing similar challenges. When Steve was tragically shot dead, the blog transformed into a lifeline for Lokita, helping her find a reason to live, a means to heal herself, and the courage to face her husband's killers.

From an early age, Lokita has cultivated her distinctive *experiential writing* style through journals, letters, real-life short stories, poetry, and essays. These mediums continue to serve as her primary tools for self-reflection and sharing insights with others. As she pursued university studies in German and English literature, linguistics, and philosophy, Lokita's writings garnered recognition, featuring in magazines and anthologies that showcased noteworthy young authors.

Lokita has written for *Huffington Post*, authored many articles on spirituality and Tantra, appeared on numerous television programs and has co-produced best-selling educational programs about Tantra.

She divides her time between California, Costa Rica, and Germany, and is working on her second book about her unique and riveting life story.

STAY IN TOUCH

Thank you for reading this memoir.
For more information about Lokita Carter and her work,
photos and more:

visit www.lokitacarter.com

If you have been touched by this story, please post a review on
Amazon or wherever you purchased this book.
It is greatly appreciated.

www.ingramcontent.com/pod-product-compliance
Lightning Source LLC
Chambersburg PA
CBHW030528010526
44110CB00048B/778